303 Simple & Satisfying Recipes

Sunrise Pizza, page 13

Country Chicken Stew, page 165

Iced Carrot Cookies, page 247

Gooseberry Patch
2500 Farmers Dr., #110
Columbus, OH 43235

www.gooseberrypatch.com
1·800·854·6673

Copyright 2013, Gooseberry Patch 978-1-62093-128-8
First Printing, June, 2013

All rights reserved. No part of this book may be reproduced or utilized in any form or by any means, electronic or mechanical, including photocopying and recording, or by any information storage and retrieval system, without permission in writing from the publisher. Printed in Korea.

Check out our cooking videos on YouTube!

Scan this code with your smartphone or tablet…it takes you right to our YouTube playlist of cooking videos for **303 Simple & Satisfying Recipes**. While there, you can also view our entire collection of **Gooseberry Patch** cooking videos!

If you spot this icon next to a recipe name, it means we created a video for it. You'll find it at **www.youtube.com/gooseberrypatchcom**

Gooseberry Patch *cookbooks*

Triple-Layered Brownies, page 275

Salmon Cornbread Cakes, page 38

Since 1992, we've been publishing our own country cookbooks for every kitchen and for every meal of the day! Each title has hundreds of budget-friendly recipes, using ingredients you already have on hand in your pantry.

In addition, you'll find helpful tips and ideas on every page, along with our hand-drawn artwork and plenty of personality. Their lay-flat binding makes them so easy to use...they're sure to become a fast favorite in your kitchen.

Call us toll-free at
1·800·854·6673
and we'd be delighted to tell you all about our newest titles!

Shop with us online anytime at
www.gooseberrypatch.com

Send us your favorite recipe!

and the memory that makes it special for you!* If we select your recipe for a brand-new **Gooseberry Patch** cookbook, your name will appear right along with it...and you'll receive a FREE copy of the book!

Submit your recipe on our website at
www.gooseberrypatch.com

Or mail to:

Gooseberry Patch • Attn: Cookbook Dept.
2500 Farmers Dr., #110 • Columbus, OH 43235

*Please include the number of servings and all other necessary information!

Have a taste for more?

Visit **www.gooseberrypatch.com** to join our **Circle of Friends**!

- Free recipes, tips and ideas plus a complete cookbook index
- Get special email offers and our monthly eLetter delivered to your inbox
- Find local stores with **Gooseberry Patch** cookbooks, calendars and organizers

CONTENTS

101 EASY EVERYDAY RECIPES

101 SLOW-COOKER RECIPES

CONTENTS

101 CUPCAKE, COOKIE & BROWNIE RECIPES

Sunday Meatball Skillet, page 45

Texas Queso Dip, page 131

Key Lime Cupcakes, page 221

Ripe Tomato Tart, page 72

Coconut-Orange Breakfast Rolls, page 10

Spicy Salsa Twists, page 41

Garden Rice Salad, page 89

101 *Easy* EVERYDAY RECIPES

Breakfast Bruschetta, page 19

White Chocolate–Butterscotch Pretzels, page 105

Sweet-and-Sour Slaw, page 84

A tasty collection of effortless and delicious dishes for breakfasts, lunches, dinners and more…plus, the cooking times are no longer than 30 minutes!

Strawberry Dessert, page 91

Asian Chicken Wraps, page 32

Jax's Cheeseburger Pizzas, page 65

Everyday Kitchen Tips

★ A pizza cutter makes quick work of dividing up casserole servings while the casserole is still in the baking pan!

★ Freeze uncooked pork chops or chicken cutlets with marinade in freezer bags. After thawing overnight in the fridge, meat can go right into the baking pan or skillet for a scrumptious meal in a jiffy.

★ The easiest-ever way to cook egg noodles...bring water to a rolling boil, then turn off heat. Add noodles and let stand for 20 minutes, stirring twice. Perfect!

★ Summer's bounty of delicious red and yellow peppers can be saved for winter enjoyment. Fill ice cube trays with diced peppers and water, then freeze. Toss frozen cubes right into simmering dishes for a burst of flavor and color.

★ Need softened butter in a jiffy? Grate sticks with a cheese grater and it will soften in just minutes!

★ If there's leftover salad after dinner, use it for a tasty sandwich filling the next day. Split a pita pocket, stuff with salad, chopped chicken or turkey, sliced grapes and drizzle with salad dressing.

Egg & Bacon Quesadillas

2 T. butter, divided
4 8-inch flour tortillas
5 eggs, beaten
1/2 c. milk
2 8-oz. pkgs. shredded
   Cheddar cheese
6 to 8 slices bacon, crisply
   cooked and crumbled
Optional: salsa, sour cream

Lightly spread about 1/4 teaspoon
butter on one side of each tortilla;
set aside. In a bowl, beat eggs and
milk until combined. Pour egg
mixture into a hot, lightly greased
skillet; cook and stir over medium
heat until done. Remove scrambled
eggs to a dish and keep warm. Melt
remaining butter in the skillet and
add a tortilla, buttered-side down.
Layer with 1/4 of the cheese, 1/2 of
the eggs and 1/2 of the bacon. Top
with 1/4 of the cheese and a tortilla,
buttered-side up. Cook one to
2 minutes on each side, until golden.
Repeat with remaining ingredients.
Cut each into 4 wedges and serve
with salsa and sour cream, if desired.
Serves 4.

9

Joshua Logan
Corpus Christi, TX
My kids raved about these
after a sleepover at their
Aunt Sherry's house.
I like to spice up mine
with hot sauce!

Coconut-Orange Breakfast Rolls

12.4-oz. tube refrigerated
　　cinnamon rolls with icing
3/4 to 1 c. sweetened flaked
　　coconut
1 t. canola oil
1/2 c. orange marmalade
1/4 c. sliced almonds
1/2 to 1 t. almond extract

Separate dough into 8 rolls; set icing aside. Place coconut in a dish. Roll each roll in coconut, pressing to make sure sides are covered. Place rolls, cinnamon-side up, into a 9" round cake pan coated with oil. Make a well in the center of each roll; fill with one tablespoon marmalade. Sprinkle rolls with almonds. Bake at 400 degrees for 15 to 20 minutes, until golden. Cool in pan 10 minutes. Mix almond extract into reserved icing. Spread rolls carefully with icing. Serve warm. Makes 8 servings.

Jewel Sharpe
Raleigh, NC

These sweet rolls are our favorite breakfast when we go camping. Just a few extra ingredients turn store-bought rolls into homemade goodies!

Savory Breakfast Pancakes

2 c. biscuit baking mix
1 c. milk
2 eggs, beaten
1/2 c. shredded mozzarella cheese
1/2 c. pepperoni, chopped
1/2 c. tomato, chopped
1/4 c. green pepper, chopped
2 t. Italian seasoning
Garnish: pizza sauce, grated
   Parmesan cheese

Stir together baking mix, milk
and eggs until well blended; add
remaining ingredients except
garnish. Heat a lightly greased
griddle over medium-high heat.
Ladle batter by 1/4 cupfuls onto the
griddle; cook until golden on both
sides. Garnish with warmed pizza
sauce and Parmesan cheese. Makes
15 pancakes.

11

Jessica Parker
Mulvane, KS

Give the kids the unexpected
for breakfast...these will
disappear fast!

Nutty Brown Sugar Muffins

2 eggs, beaten
1/2 c. butter, melted and cooled slightly
1 c. brown sugar, packed
1/2 c. all-purpose flour
1 c. chopped pecans

Stir together eggs and butter. Add remaining ingredients; stir just until blended. Spray foil muffin cup liners with non-stick vegetable spray. Place liners in a muffin tin; fill 2/3 full. Bake at 350 degrees for 25 minutes. Remove muffins from pan immediately; cool. Makes 10.

Pearl Weaver
East Prairie, MO
With a flavor that's so much like pecan pie, these muffins are sure to become a new favorite.

Sunrise Pizza

8-oz. tube refrigerated
    crescent rolls
1 c. cooked ham, diced
1 c. frozen diced potatoes with
    onions and peppers
1 c. shredded sharp Cheddar
    cheese
4 eggs
3 T. milk
1/2 t. salt
1/4 t. pepper

Separate rolls into 4 rectangles.
Place on an ungreased baking sheet
or 12" round pizza pan. Build up
edges slightly to form a crust. Firmly
press perforations to seal. Sprinkle
ham evenly over crust. Top with
frozen vegetables and cheese. Beat
eggs; stir in milk, salt and pepper.
Pour egg mixture over cheese in
crust. Bake at 375 degrees for 15
minutes, or until center is set. Cut
into wedges to serve. Serves 6.

13

Mary Lou Thomas
Portland, ME

A quick recipe just right
for busy mornings. We wrap
up individual slices and pop
them in the microwave before
heading out the door!

Apple-Stuffed French Toast

3 apples, peeled, cored and cut
    into chunks
1/4 c. brown sugar, packed
cinnamon to taste
2 eggs, beaten
1/2 c. milk
1 t. vanilla extract
8 slices wheat bread
Garnish: maple syrup

In a microwave-safe bowl, combine
apples, brown sugar and cinnamon.
Cover and microwave on high for
5 minutes, until apples are soft. In a
separate bowl, stir together eggs, milk
and vanilla. Spray a griddle or large
frying pan with non-stick vegetable
spray and heat over medium heat.
Quickly dip the bread on both sides
in the egg mixture and place on the
griddle. Cook until golden on both
sides. Place one slice of toast on a
plate; put a scoop of the apple mixture
in the middle. Top with another slice
of toast. Drizzle with maple syrup.
Makes 4 servings.

Wendy Paffenroth
Pine Island, NY

Amazing aroma and divine
flavor...that's what
breakfast is all about!

Kitchen Café Mocha

6 c. hot brewed coffee
3/4 c. half-and-half
6 T. chocolate syrup
2 T. plus 1 t. sugar
Garnish: whipped cream,
    chocolate syrup

In a large saucepan, combine all
ingredients except garnish. Cook
and stir over medium heat until sugar
is dissolved and mixture is heated
through. Pour into mugs and garnish
as desired. Makes 6 servings.

15

Carrie O'Shea
Marina Del Rey, CA
Oh, café mocha is such a
treat! I make this every
Saturday to tote with me
on errands.

Peachy Waffle Topping

16-oz. can sliced peaches in
　heavy syrup
1 T. lemon juice
1 T. cornstarch

Strain syrup from peaches into a
saucepan. Cut peaches into bite-size
pieces and set aside. In a bowl, mix
lemon juice with cornstarch. Stir
lemon mixture into syrup in saucepan.
Cook and stir over medium heat for
one minute, or until thickened. Stir
in peach slices. Makes about 2 cups.

Tori Willis
Champaign, IL

I recently tried this recipe
for the first time...after
one bite, I thought,
"I've got to share this
with all my friends!"

No-Cook Strawberry Freezer Jam

7 c. strawberries, hulled
1-3/4 oz. pkg. light powdered
    pectin
1-3/4 c. sugar, divided
1 c. light corn syrup
8 1/2-pint freezer-safe plastic
    containers and lids, sterilized

Thoroughly crush strawberries in a large bowl; set aside. Combine pectin with 1/4 cup sugar. Gradually add pectin mixture to strawberries, stirring vigorously. Let stand for 30 minutes, stirring occasionally. Add corn syrup; mix well. Gradually stir in remaining sugar until dissolved. Spoon into containers leaving 1/2-inch headspace; secure lids. Let stand overnight at room temperature before freezing. May be frozen up to one year. Store in refrigerator up to 4 weeks after opening. Makes 8 containers.

17

Dianne Gregory
Sheridan, AR

It's so simple to preserve the sunny taste of fresh strawberries! Spread over hot biscuits, toast or yogurt.

Buttermilk Oven Pancakes

1-1/2 c. all-purpose flour
2 T. sugar
1 t. baking soda
1 t. baking powder
1/4 t. salt
1 egg, beaten
1-1/2 c. buttermilk
3 T. oil
cinnamon-sugar to taste
Garnish: butter, maple syrup

In a bowl, stir together flour, sugar, baking soda, baking powder and salt. In a separate bowl, combine egg, buttermilk and oil; add to dry ingredients. Stir just until mixed, but lightly lumpy. Spread batter evenly in a greased and floured 15"x10" jelly-roll pan. Sprinkle with cinnamon-sugar to taste. Bake at 350 degrees for 16 to 18 minutes, until top springs back when lightly touched and edges are lightly golden. Cut into squares and serve with butter and maple syrup. Makes 4 to 6 servings.

Cindy Lyzenga
Zeeland, MI

What I like best about this recipe is no one has to stand by the stove and flip pancakes! For a different taste, sprinkle the batter with fresh fruit.

Breakfast Bruschetta

1 c. red or green grapes, sliced
1 c. strawberries, hulled and
   sliced
1/4 t. cinnamon
1/8 t. nutmeg
1 c. cottage cheese or ricotta
1 T. chopped walnuts
1 baguette, cut in half lengthwise
   and sliced into 1-inch
   diagonals
2 to 3 T. olive oil

Place fruit in a small bowl; sprinkle with cinnamon and nutmeg. In another bowl, mix cheese and nuts. Brush bread lightly with olive oil and place on an ungreased baking sheet. Bake at 450 degrees until the bread turns golden, about 3 minutes. Remove from oven and spread cheese mixture on each piece of bread. Top with fruit mixture. Serves 4.

19

Jill Ball
Highland, UT

My family loves bruschetta,
so I thought, why not
have it for breakfast?

Slow-Cooker Hashbrown Casserole

32-oz. pkg. frozen shredded
    hashbrowns
1 lb. ground pork sausage,
    browned and drained
1 onion, diced
1 green pepper, diced
1-1/2 c. shredded Cheddar cheese
1 doz. eggs, beaten
1 c. milk
1 t. salt
1 t. pepper

Place 1/3 each of hashbrowns, sausage,
onion, green pepper and cheese in a
lightly greased slow cooker. Repeat
layering 2 more times, ending with
cheese. Beat eggs, milk, salt and pepper
together in a large bowl; pour over top.
Cover and cook on low setting for
10 hours. Serves 8.

Jessica Robertson
Fishers, IN

Sometimes I'll substitute
bacon or ham in place of the
sausage. This hearty recipe
works best in a large,
oval slow-cooker.

Ham & Feta Cheese Omelet

2 eggs, beaten
1/4 c. crumbled feta cheese
1/4 c. cucumber, diced
2 T. green onion, chopped
1/4 c. cooked ham, cubed
salt and pepper to taste
Garnish: salsa

Combine all ingredients except
salsa in a bowl; mix well. Pour into
a lightly greased sauté pan or small
skillet. Without stirring, cook over
low heat until set. Fold over; transfer
to serving plate. Serve with salsa.
Makes one serving.

21

Holly Jackson
Saint George, UT

All I can say
is, "Mmm!"

Good Morning Blueberry Shake

Jo Ann

I enjoy a yummy
breakfast shake...this
drink blends up fast
and is so pretty!

2-1/2 c. blueberries
1-1/4 c. apple juice
1 c. frozen vanilla yogurt
1/4 c. milk
3/4 t. cinnamon
Garnish: additional blueberries

Combine all ingredients except garnish
in a blender and process until smooth.
Garnish with additional blueberries.
Serve immediately. Makes 4 servings.

Easiest Cinnamon-Raisin Rolls

2 c. biscuit baking mix
1/2 c. raisins
1/2 c. sour cream
4 T. milk, divided
2 T. butter, softened
1/2 c. brown sugar, packed
1/4 c. nuts, finely chopped
1/2 t. cinnamon
1 c. powdered sugar

In a bowl, stir baking mix, raisins, sour cream and 3 tablespoons milk, just until combined. Gently smooth dough into a ball on a floured tea towel. Knead 10 times. Roll dough into a 12-inch by 10-inch rectangle. Spread rectangle with softened butter. Mix brown sugar, nuts and cinnamon; sprinkle over dough. Starting on the long end, roll up dough tightly; pinch edge to seal. Cut roll into 12 slices. Place slices, cut-side down, in greased muffin cups. Bake at 400 degrees for 15 minutes, or until golden. Stir together remaining milk and powdered sugar; drizzle over warm rolls. Makes one dozen.

23

Nola Coons
Gooseberry Patch
Brew a pot of coffee and share these wonderful rolls with your neighborhood pals.

Butterscotch Coffee Cake

18-1/2 oz. pkg. yellow cake mix
3.4-oz. pkg. instant vanilla
   pudding mix
3.4-oz. pkg. instant butterscotch
   pudding mix
4 eggs, beaten
1/2 c. oil
1 c. water
3/4 c. brown sugar, packed
3/4 c. chopped walnuts
1 t. cinnamon

With an electric mixer on medium speed, combine dry cake mix, dry pudding mixes, eggs, oil and water. Pour into a greased 13"x9" baking pan. Combine remaining ingredients and sprinkle over cake. Bake at 350 degrees for 40 minutes, or until toothpick tests clean. Let cool and cut into squares. Makes 12 servings.

Luann Hartzler
Creston, OH

A neighbor brought this coffee cake as a house-warming gift twenty years ago and it's been a favorite ever since. Moist and very flavorful!

Scott's Wonderful Waffles

1 c. milk
1/2 c. oil
3 eggs, beaten
1-1/2 c. cherry pie filling
18-1/2 oz. pkg. yellow cake mix
Garnish: butter, maple syrup

In a bowl, mix all ingredients except garnish. Refrigerate until waffle iron is ready. Ladle batter by 1/2 cupfuls onto a lightly greased preheated waffle iron; bake according to manufacturer's directions. Garnish as desired. Makes 8 to 10 waffles.

Sheila Murray
Tehachapi, CA

My son came up with this recipe and made it for the whole family. It was a great hit!

Trail Mix Bagels

8-oz. pkg. cream cheese, softened
1 T. lemon juice
1 t. lemon zest, grated
1/2 c. raisins
1 carrot, peeled and grated
1/3 c. trail mix, coarsely chopped,
   or sunflower kernels
4 bagels, split

Place cream cheese in a bowl. Add remaining ingredients except bagels; stir until well blended and creamy. Spread between sliced bagels and wrap up for the trail. Makes 4 servings.

Becky Drees
Pittsfield, MA

Perfect for an on-the-go breakfast, lunch or hike... a tasty energy boost!

Sweet & Spicy Bacon

1/2 c. brown sugar, packed
2 T. chili powder
1 t. ground cumin
1 t. cumin seed
1 t. ground coriander
1/4 t. cayenne pepper
10 thick slices bacon

Line a 15"x10" jelly-roll pan with aluminum foil. Place a wire rack on pan and set aside. Combine all ingredients except bacon; sprinkle mixture onto a large piece of wax paper. Press bacon into mixture, turning to coat well. Arrange in a single layer on prepared pan; place pan on center rack of oven. Bake at 400 degrees for 12 minutes; turn bacon over. Bake for an additional 10 minutes, until deep golden. Drain on paper towels; serve warm. Serves 4 to 5.

27

Zoe Bennett
Columbia, SC

Try this easy-to-fix bacon at your next brunch...guests will love it!

Cream Cheesy Strudel

2 8-oz. tubes refrigerated crescent
  rolls, divided
2 8-oz. pkgs. cream cheese,
  softened
1 egg, beaten
1/2 c. plus 2 T. sugar, divided
1 t. vanilla extract
1/4 t. cinnamon

Arrange one tube crescent rolls in the
bottom of an ungreased 13"x9" baking
pan. Mix cream cheese, egg, 1/2 cup
sugar and vanilla; spread over crescent
rolls. Cover with remaining crescent
rolls; sprinkle with cinnamon and
remaining sugar. Bake at 375 degrees
for 11 to 13 minutes. Cut into squares
to serve. Makes 1-1/2 to 2 dozen.

Donna Simonson
Sullivan, OH

Dress up this strudel for
the holidays! Just sprinkle
with colored sugar...red and
green for Christmas, yellow
and pink for Easter.

Make-Ahead Cheese & Egg Casserole

3 c. seasoned croutons
15 eggs, beaten
2 c. milk
1 t. seasoned salt
1 t. pepper
3/4 t. onion powder
2 T. fresh chives, chopped
1-1/2 c. shredded Cheddar
   cheese

Place croutons in a 13"x9" baking pan coated with non-stick vegetable spray. Whisk together eggs, milk and seasonings; stir in cheese. Pour over croutons. Cover and chill 8 hours, stirring once. Uncover and stir. Bake at 350 degrees for 30 minutes, or until set. Serves 8 to 10.

Irene Robinson
Cincinnati, OH

This overnight casserole is great for weekend breakfasts or a special brunch.

Balsamic Chicken & Pears

2 t. oil, divided
4 boneless, skinless chicken breasts
2 Bosc pears, cored and cut into
   8 wedges
1 c. chicken broth
3 T. balsamic vinegar
2 t. cornstarch
1-1/2 t. sugar
1/4 c. dried cherries or raisins

Heat one teaspoon oil in a large non-stick skillet over medium-high heat; add chicken. Cook until golden and cooked through, about 4 to 5 minutes per side. Transfer to a plate; keep warm. Heat remaining oil in same skillet; add pears and cook until tender and golden. In a small bowl, combine remaining ingredients except cherries or raisins. Stir broth mixture into skillet with pears; add cherries or raisins. Bring to a boil over medium heat. Cook for one minute, stirring constantly. Return chicken to pan; heat through. Serve pear sauce over chicken. Serves 4.

Shirl Parsons
Cape Carteret, NC

The flavors in this dish blend together so well... very, very tasty!

Italian Sausage Skillet

1-1/4 lb. pkg. Italian pork
   sausage links
3 zucchini, cubed
1/2 c. onion, chopped
14-1/2 oz. can stewed tomatoes
cooked pasta

In a skillet over medium heat, cook
sausage until no longer pink; drain.
Cut sausage into 1/4-inch slices;
return to skillet and cook until
browned. Add zucchini and onion;
cook and stir for 2 minutes. Stir
in tomatoes with juice. Reduce
heat; cover and simmer for 10 to
15 minutes, until zucchini is
tender. Serve over cooked pasta.
Serves 4 to 6.

31

Mary Gage
Wakewood, CA
Such a versatile dish...use
a combination of yellow
squash and zucchini
or serve over rice.

Asian Chicken Wraps

2 boneless, skinless chicken
   breasts, cooked and shredded
2/3 c. General Tso's sauce
1/4 c. teriyaki sauce
4 10-inch flour tortillas
10-oz. pkg. romaine and cabbage
   salad mix
1/2 c. carrot, peeled and shredded
1/4 c. sliced almonds
2 T. chow mein noodles

Combine chicken and sauces in a
skillet. Cook over medium heat until
heated through; remove from heat.
Divide ingredients evenly on each
tortilla, beginning with salad mix,
carrot, chicken mixture, almonds and
ending with chow mein noodles. Roll
up burrito style. Makes 4 servings.

Lisa Stanish
Houston, TX

These wraps are very easy
to prepare after a long day
at work. They're so much
tastier than fast food!

Jambalaya in a Jiff

2 T. butter
7-oz. pkg. chicken-flavored rice
    vermicelli mix
2-3/4 c. water
1/4 t. pepper
1/4 t. hot pepper sauce
1 T. dried, minced onion
1/4 c. celery, diced
1/4 c. green pepper, diced
2 c. cooked ham, diced
1 lb. cooked medium shrimp

Melt butter in a large saucepan over medium heat. Add rice vermicelli mix and sauté just until golden. Stir in remaining ingredients; reduce heat, cover and simmer for 15 minutes. Serves 4 to 6.

33

Patricia Perkins
Shenandoah, IA

Add a little more
hot pepper sauce if
you like it spicy!

Key West Burgers

1 lb. ground beef
3 T. Key lime juice
1/4 c. fresh cilantro, chopped
salt and pepper to taste
hamburger buns, split and toasted
Garnish: lettuce

In a bowl, combine ground beef, lime juice, cilantro, salt and pepper. Form beef mixture into 4 patties. Spray a large skillet with non-stick vegetable spray. Cook patties over medium heat for 6 minutes. Flip patties, cover skillet and cook for another 6 minutes. Place lettuce on bottom halves of buns and top with patties. Add Creamy Burger Spread onto bun tops and close sandwiches. Serves 4.

Creamy Burger Spread:

8-oz. pkg. cream cheese, softened
8-oz. container sour cream
3 green onion tops, chopped

Combine all ingredients until completely blended. Cover and refrigerate at least 15 minutes.

Kimberly Ascroft
Merritt Island, FL

For a real Key West experience, enjoy these flavorful burgers with a frozen tropical drink!

Unstuffed Green Pepper Soup

2 lbs. ground beef
2 10-3/4 oz. cans tomato soup
28-oz. can petite diced tomatoes
4-oz. can mushroom pieces,
    drained
2 c. green peppers, diced
1 c. onion, diced
1/4 c. brown sugar, packed
3 to 4 c. beef broth
2 c. cooked rice

In a stockpot over medium heat,
brown ground beef; drain. Stir in
soup, vegetables and brown sugar.
Add desired amount of beef broth.
Simmer, covered, until peppers and
onion are tender, about 30 minutes.
Stir in rice about 5 minutes before
serving. Makes 8 servings.

35

Peggy Cantrell
Okmulgee, OK

This soup is right up
there on my list of comfort
foods! All the flavors of
a stuffed green pepper
without the work.

Company's Coming Pork Chops

4 to 6 boneless pork chops
salt and pepper to taste
1/4 c. olive oil
1 c. white wine or chicken broth
4 to 5 green onions, chopped
1 t. dried thyme
1 c. milk
1 t. cornstarch

Season pork chops with salt and pepper. Heat oil in a skillet over medium-high heat. Brown pork chops on both sides, turning once; drain. Add wine or broth to the pan and use a wooden spoon to scrape up the drippings. Stir in onions and thyme. Reduce heat to medium-low and simmer until liquid is reduced, about 5 minutes. Whisk milk and cornstarch together and pour over chops. Simmer, stirring occasionally for 15 minutes, or until sauce is thickened. Remove chops from pan; serve with sauce. Serves 4 to 6.

Nancy Cowling
DeQueen, AR
I love to make this recipe on a busy weeknight. Tastes and looks special, but it's fast and easy!

Easy Skillet Lasagna

1-1/2 T. olive oil
1/2 green pepper, finely chopped
1 onion, finely chopped
1 clove garlic, minced
16-oz. jar spaghetti sauce
1 lb. ground beef, browned and
    drained
6 lasagna noodles, cooked and
    cut in half
12-oz. container small-curd
    cottage cheese
4 slices mozzarella cheese
1/2 c. Parmesan cheese

37

Heat oil in a skillet over medium heat. Sauté green pepper, onion and garlic until tender; drain. Transfer to a bowl; stir in spaghetti sauce and browned beef. In skillet, layer 1/3 of sauce mixture, half the lasagna noodles, half the cottage cheese, 2 slices of mozzarella and half the Parmesan. Repeat layers. Top with remaining sauce, making sure to cover all noodles. Cover and simmer over medium-low heat for 10 to 15 minutes. Remove from heat and let stand for 10 minutes before uncovering and serving. Serves 4.

Terri McClure
Hilliard, OH

My husband often asks me to make this recipe. And sometimes, he even helps prepare it! Tastes great with ground turkey too.

Salmon Cornbread Cakes

2 T. mayonnaise
2 eggs, beaten
1 t. dried parsley
3 green onions, thinly sliced
1 t. seafood seasoning
1 to 2 t. Worcestershire sauce
14-3/4 oz. can salmon, drained
   and bones removed
2 c. cornbread, crumbled
1 T. canola oil

Combine mayonnaise, eggs, parsley, green onions, seafood seasoning and Worcestershire sauce. Mix well. Mix in salmon and cornbread. Shape into 6 to 8 patties. Heat oil in a skillet over medium heat. Cook patties for 3 to 4 minutes on each side, until golden. Serves 6.

Lorrie Smith
Drummonds, TN

A different take on traditional salmon croquettes. I absolutely love these!

Hug in a Mug Soup

1 lb. ground turkey
1 T. butter
1 onion, chopped
3 cloves garlic, minced
1 green pepper, chopped
1.35-oz. pkg. onion soup mix
16-oz. can navy beans, drained
   and rinsed
16-oz. can kidney beans, drained
   and rinsed
28-oz. can crushed tomatoes
28-oz. can diced tomatoes,
   drained
1 T. dried parsley
1 T. dried basil
8 c. water
salt and pepper to taste
1 c. small pasta shells, uncooked

In a stockpot over medium heat, brown turkey; drain and set aside. In the same pot, melt butter over medium heat; sauté onion, garlic and green pepper until tender. Add remaining ingredients except pasta and bring to a boil. Stir in pasta. Simmer, uncovered, over medium heat for 10 minutes, or until pasta is tender. Serves 8.

Michelle Marberry
Valley, AL

A quick-to-fix family favorite! Serve in big soup mugs with a hearty bread for a very comforting supper.

Saucy Slow-Cooker Pulled Pork

1 T. barbecue spice rub
4-lb. boneless pork shoulder
1-1/2 yellow onions, sliced
2 16-oz. cans whole-berry
    cranberry sauce
18-oz. bottle barbecue sauce
6 to 8 sandwich rolls, split

Pat spice rub onto pork shoulder. Wrap pork in plastic wrap and refrigerate overnight. Add onions to a slow cooker and place unwrapped pork on top. In a bowl, combine cranberry sauce and barbecue sauce. Pour sauce mixture over pork. Cover and cook on low setting for 8 to 10 hours. Remove pork to a bowl and shred with 2 forks. Strain about 1-1/2 cups sauce from the slow cooker and stir into shredded pork. Serve on sandwich rolls. Serves 6 to 8.

Karen Christiansen
Glenview, IL

I overheard part of this recipe while standing in the checkout line at the grocery store! I only knew some ingredients, so I came up with my own version.

Spicy Salsa Twists

1 lb. ground beef, browned and
   drained
8-oz. pkg. rotini pasta, cooked
10-3/4 oz. can tomato soup
1 c. salsa
1/2 c. milk
1 c. shredded Cheddar cheese,
   divided
Optional: sour cream, tortilla
   chips

Combine browned beef, rotini,
soup, salsa, milk and 1/2 cup cheese
in a large skillet. Cook over medium
heat until heated through and cheese
is melted; sprinkle with remaining
cheese. Serve with sour cream and
tortilla chips, if desired. Serves 5.

41

Heather Jacobson
Galesville, WI

A wonderful dish that's
big on flavor and cooks up
in a snap!

Skillet Dinner

1 lb. ground beef
1 onion, chopped
14-1/2 oz. can beef broth
2/3 c. water
1 c. long-cooking rice, uncooked
1/2 t. dry mustard
1 green pepper, chopped
1 tomato, chopped
1 c. shredded Pepper Jack cheese

Brown ground beef and onion in a large skillet over medium heat; drain. Stir in broth, water, rice and dry mustard; bring to a boil. Reduce heat; simmer, uncovered, until liquid is absorbed, about 25 minutes. Stir in green pepper and tomato; sprinkle cheese over top. Cover and remove from heat. Let stand for 2 to 3 minutes, until cheese melts. Serves 4 to 6.

Denise Oravecz
Pittsburgh, PA

Hearty and filling...a real family-pleaser!

Mandy's Hand-Battered Chicken

1-1/2 lbs. boneless, skinless
    chicken breast tenders
3 c. self-rising flour
2 T. salt
1 T. pepper
2 t. garlic powder
dried parsley to taste
2 c. cold milk
oil for deep frying
Optional: additional dried
    parsley

Pat chicken dry. Combine flour and seasonings in a large bowl. Add milk to a separate bowl. Working with several pieces at a time, dip chicken into milk and then dredge in flour mixture. Set aside. Cover the bottom of a 12" skillet with oil; heat over medium heat until hot, about 3 to 4 minutes. Place chicken tenders in skillet and fry until crisp on one side; turn over. Continue frying until golden and crisp on all sides and juices run clear when chicken is pierced with a fork. Be careful not to overcook. Remove from skillet and drain on a paper-towel lined plate. Garnish with additional parsley, if desired. Serves 4.

43

Amanda Johnson
Marysville, OH

This is a recipe I whipped up one day when our pantry was running low with supplies. It's simple but makes the best chicken tenders. Dip in your favorite sauce!

Lemony "Baked" Chicken

3 to 4-lb. roasting chicken
2 T. olive oil
1 lemon
2 cloves garlic, minced
1 t. dried parsley
salt and pepper to taste

Pat chicken dry with a paper towel; rub with oil. Put whole lemon inside chicken; place in a slow cooker. Sprinkle with seasonings. Cover and cook on high setting for one hour. Turn to low setting and cook an additional 6 to 7 hours. Makes 4 servings.

Sharon Lundberg
Longwood, FL
Stir a little lemon zest and chopped parsley into steamed rice for a perfect side dish. Choose a large, oval slow cooker for this recipe.

Sunday Meatball Skillet

3/4 lb. ground beef
1 c. onion, grated
1/2 c. Italian-flavored dry bread
  crumbs
1 egg, beaten
1/4 c. catsup
1/4 t. pepper
2 c. beef broth
1/4 c. all-purpose flour
1/2 c. sour cream
8-oz. pkg. medium egg noodles,
  cooked
Garnish: chopped fresh parsley

In a bowl, combine beef, onion, bread crumbs, egg, catsup and pepper. Shape into one-inch meatballs. Spray a skillet with non-stick vegetable spray. Cook meatballs over medium heat, turning occasionally, until browned, about 10 minutes. Remove meatballs and let drain on paper towels. In a bowl, whisk together broth and flour; add to skillet. Cook and stir until mixture thickens, about 5 minutes. Stir in sour cream. Add meatballs and noodles; toss to coat. Cook and stir until heated through, about 5 minutes. Garnish with parsley. Serves 4.

Doris Stegner
Gooseberry Patch

Oh-so delicious alongside roasted green beans and a bowl of homemade applesauce!

45

Penne & Spring Vegetables

16-oz. pkg. penne pasta, uncooked
1 lb. asparagus, cut into 1/2-inch
    pieces
1/2 lb. sugar snap peas
3 T. olive oil
1/2 c. grated Parmesan cheese
salt and pepper to taste

Cook pasta according to package
directions. Add asparagus during the
last 4 minutes of cook time; add peas
during the last 2 minutes of cook time.
Remove pot from heat; drain pasta
mixture and return to pot. Toss with
remaining ingredients; serve warm.
Serves 4 to 6.

Denise Piccirilli
Huber Heights, OH

A delicious meatless main
or a tasty side for
grilled chicken.

Chicken & Peppers Stir-Fry

1/2 c. soy sauce
2 T. sesame oil
1 T. catsup
4 cloves garlic, minced
4 boneless, skinless chicken
    breasts, cut into 1-inch pieces
1/2 red pepper, chopped
1/2 yellow pepper, chopped
cooked rice

In a bowl, whisk together soy sauce, oil, catsup and garlic. Heat mixture in a skillet over medium-high heat. Add chicken; cook and stir for 3 minutes. Add peppers; cook and stir 5 minutes, or until chicken is cooked through. Serve over hot rice. Serves 4.

47

Regina Wickline
Pebble Beach, CA

I was inspired to create this colorful and yummy recipe after falling in love with a similar dish at my favorite downtown restaurant.

Apple-Stuffed Turkey Breast

1-1/2 c. long grain & wild rice,
   uncooked
2 apples, peeled, cored and
   chopped
1 onion, finely chopped
1/2 c. sweetened dried cranberries
3 c. water
4 to 5-lb. boneless, skinless turkey
   breast

Combine rice, apples, onion and
cranberries in a slow cooker; pour
water over top. Mix well. Place turkey
on top of rice mixture. Cover and
cook on low setting for 8 to 9 hours.
Serves 10.

Dale Duncan
Waterloo, IA

The combination of wild rice,
apples and cranberries
really gives this turkey
an amazing flavor.

Hearty Chicken-Bacon Melts

4 boneless, skinless chicken
    breasts
1 onion, sliced
2 t. margarine
2 t. olive oil
4 slices bread, toasted
4 t. steak sauce
8 slices bacon, crisply cooked
1 c. shredded Cheddar cheese

Place chicken between pieces of wax paper and flatten to about 1/4-inch thickness. In a large skillet, cook onion in margarine and oil until softened. Remove onion from skillet. Add chicken to skillet; cook for about 7 to 9 minutes on each side, until cooked through. Place toasted bread slices on a large baking sheet; spread each slice with one teaspoon steak sauce. Top each with a chicken breast, 2 slices bacon, 1/4 of onion slices and 1/4 cup cheese. Broil 4 to 6 inches from heat for one to 2 minutes, until cheese is melted. Serves 4.

49

Vickie

A warm, melty open-face
sandwich you need to
eat with a fork!

Creamy Chicken Bake

2 c. elbow macaroni, uncooked
1 c. mayonnaise
10-3/4 oz. can cream of chicken
    soup
1-1/2 c. cooked chicken, chopped
2 c. grated Parmesan cheese
1/4 c. chopped pimentos
1/4 c. onion, chopped
1/2 c. potato chips, crushed

Cook macaroni according to package
instructions; drain. Meanwhile, in a
bowl, combine mayonnaise, soup
and chicken. Stir in macaroni and
remaining ingredients except potato
chips. Transfer to a lightly greased
13"x9" baking pan; sprinkle with
potato chips. Bake, uncovered, at
375 degrees for 30 minutes, or
until bubbly. Serves 4 to 6.

April Jacobs
Loveland, CO

When my picky eaters
are away, I'll stir
in my favorite
ingredients...mushrooms
and chopped green pepper!

Chili & Biscuits

Lisa Hains
Ontario, Canada

This dish was created by combining two family favorites into one easy dinner. If you're in a hurry, bake the biscuits separately while the chili is simmering.

1 lb. ground beef
1 onion, chopped
4 stalks celery, chopped
1-1/4 oz. pkg. chili seasoning mix
1/4 c. all-purpose flour
28-oz. can diced tomatoes
15-1/2 oz. can chili beans
Optional: 4-oz. can sliced
    mushrooms, drained
garlic powder and salt and
    pepper to taste

In a large skillet, brown together beef, onion and celery. Drain; stir in chili seasoning and flour. Add remaining ingredients and simmer until thickened and bubbly. Transfer to a lightly greased 13"x9" baking pan. Drop Biscuit Dough by tablespoonfuls over the hot chili. Bake, uncovered, at 375 degrees for 10 to 15 minutes, until biscuits are golden. Serves 6 to 8.

Biscuit Dough:

1-1/2 c. all-purpose flour
1 c. yellow cornmeal
4 t. baking powder
1/2 t. salt
2 T. sugar
1/2 c. oil
1/2 to 3/4 c. milk

Combine dry ingredients and oil. Stir in enough milk to form a soft dough.

51

Poor Man's Steak & Vegetables

6 ground beef patties
4 potatoes, peeled and cubed
3 carrots, peeled and diced
1 onion, quartered or sliced
salt and pepper to taste

Place patties in a greased 13"x9" baking pan. Evenly arrange vegetables over patties. Sprinkle with salt and pepper to taste. Bake, covered, at 400 degrees for 45 to 50 minutes, or until beef is no longer pink and potatoes are tender. Serves 6.

Cynthia Armstrong
Big Stone Gap, VA

This recipe has been handed down for several generations. My mother used to serve this dish when money was tight. It has become a family favorite!

Zippy Broiled Catfish

6 catfish fillets
1/4 c. lemon juice
1 t. salt
1/8 t. pepper
1 c. all-purpose flour
1-1/3 c. Italian salad dressing

Brush fillets with lemon juice;
sprinkle with salt and pepper.
Dredge fillets in flour. Arrange on
a well-greased broiler pan; brush
with salad dressing. Broil about
4 inches from heat source for 4 to
6 minutes, basting occasionally
with salad dressing. Turn carefully;
brush with additional salad dressing.
Broil for an additional 4 to
6 minutes, until fish flakes easily.
Serves 6.

53

Mardell Ross
Genoa, IL
Pop this in the oven and
by the time you toss the
salad and set the table,
dinner is served!

Parmesan Baked Chicken

1/2 c. butter, melted
1 clove garlic, minced
1 c. Italian-flavored dry bread
   crumbs
1/3 c. grated Parmesan cheese
2 T. fresh parsley
1/4 t. salt
1/4 t. garlic powder
pepper to taste
Optional: 1/2 t. Italian seasoning
4 to 6 boneless, skinless chicken
   breasts

In a bowl, combine butter and garlic.
In another bowl, combine bread
crumbs, Parmesan cheese and
seasonings. Dip chicken in butter
mixture to coat; dredge in bread
crumb mixture. Place chicken into an
ungreased 13"x9" baking pan. Drizzle
remaining butter mixture over chicken.
Bake, uncovered, at 400 degrees for
20 to 25 minutes, until juices run clear
when pierced. Makes 4 to 6 servings.

Gina Powell
Gadsden, AL

I tried this hand-me-down
recipe when I was looking for
something different to make
with chicken. The bottom of
the chicken will be more
browned than the top.

Cheesy Ham & Vegetable Bake

1-1/2 c. rotini pasta, uncooked
16-oz. pkg. frozen broccoli,
    carrots and cauliflower blend
1/2 c. sour cream
1/2 c. milk
1-1/2 c. shredded Cheddar
    cheese, divided
1-1/2 c. cooked ham, chopped
1/4 c. onion, chopped
1 clove garlic, minced
1/2 c. croutons, crushed

Cook pasta according to package
directions; add frozen vegetables
to cooking water just to thaw. Drain;
place mixture in a 2-quart casserole
dish that has been sprayed with
non-stick vegetable spray. Mix sour
cream, milk, one cup cheese, ham,
onion and garlic; stir into pasta
mixture in dish. Bake, uncovered, at
350 degrees for 30 minutes. Sprinkle
with croutons and remaining cheese
during last 5 minutes of baking.
Serves 6.

Jackie Flood
Geneseo, NY
A good way to use up leftover
ham after Easter or other
holiday occasions! If you
prefer a lighter version,
low-fat or fat-free products
work fine in this recipe.

Foil-Wrapped Baked Salmon

4 salmon fillets
1 onion, sliced
1/4 c. butter, diced
1 lemon, thinly sliced
1/4 c. brown sugar, packed

Place each fillet on a piece of
aluminum foil that has been sprayed
with non-stick vegetable spray. Top
fillets evenly with onion slices, diced
butter, lemon slices and brown sugar.
Fold over aluminum foil tightly to
make packets; make several holes in
top of packets with a fork to allow
steam to escape. Arrange packets on
an ungreased baking sheet. Bake at
375 degrees for 15 to 20 minutes.
Serves 4.

Katherine Murnane
Plattsburgh, NY

These packets can also
be cooked on a hot grill.
Delightful with a salad
of fresh garden greens.

Beef & Potato Roll

2 lbs. ground beef
2 t. salt
1/8 t. pepper
1 T. Worcestershire sauce
1 onion, chopped
1 egg, slightly beaten
3 slices bacon, crisply cooked
   and crumbled
3 c. mashed potatoes

In a bowl, combine all ingredients except potatoes, mixing well. Place mixture onto wax paper and shape into a rectangle approximately 1/4" thick. Mound potatoes down the center of the rectangle. Use the edges of the wax paper to wrap beef around the potatoes. Press beef edges together to seal tightly. Place roll, seam-side down, into an ungreased 11"x7" baking pan; remove wax paper. Bake, uncovered, at 350 degrees for 35 to 40 minutes, or until beef is done. Slice into portions. Serves 6 to 8.

57

Andrea Ford
Montfort, WI

This recipe was handed down from my grandma. My mom used to double the recipe for the farmhands during haying season.

Easy Sweet-and-Sour Chicken

8-oz. bottle Russian salad dressing
1-1/2 oz. pkg. onion soup mix
1/3 c. apricot jam
2-1/2 to 3 lbs. boneless, skinless
chicken breasts
Optional: chopped green onions

Whisk first 3 ingredients in a mixing bowl; set aside. Arrange chicken in an ungreased 13"x9" baking pan; pour dressing mixture on top. Bake, covered, at 350 degrees for 50 minutes to one hour, until juices run clear when chicken is pierced with a fork. If desired, cut chicken into strips before serving and garnish with green onions. Makes 4 to 6 servings.

Sandra Nakagawa
Honolulu, HI
Served on a bed of rice or crunchy chow mein noodles, this is a meal the whole family will love.

Dill Rice & Chicken

1-1/2 c. sour cream
2 10-3/4 oz. cans cream of
   chicken soup
2-1/2 c. cooked chicken, diced
1-1/2 c. quick-cooking rice,
   uncooked
1 c. shredded Cheddar cheese
1 t. poppy seed
1-1/4 t. dill weed
1/4 t. onion salt
1/4 t. garlic salt

59

Combine all ingredients and transfer to an ungreased 13"x9" baking pan. Bake, uncovered, at 350 degrees for 20 minutes. Sprinkle with Crumb Topping and bake 10 minutes longer. Makes 10 to 12 servings.

Crumb Topping:

Optional: 1/2 c. sliced almonds,
   toasted
1-1/2 c. buttery rectangular
   crackers, crushed
1/2 c. butter, melted

Combine all ingredients.

Elisabeth Miller
Rocky Mount, VA
This creamy casserole makes a great dish to carry on a picnic or even to a potluck.

Apricot-Glazed Ham Steaks

1/4 c. apricot preserves
1 T. mustard
1 t. lemon juice
1/8 t. cinnamon
4 ham steaks

In a small saucepan, combine all ingredients except ham. Cook and stir over low heat for 2 to 3 minutes. Place ham in a lightly greased 13"x9" baking dish. Pour sauce over ham. Bake, uncovered, at 350 degrees for 15 minutes, or until heated through. Serve ham topped with sauce from the pan. Makes 4 servings.

Kelly Alderson
Erie, PA

When it's grilling season, heat the ham over hot coals and serve with grilled apricot halves...oh-so good!

Down-Home Taco Casserole

1 lb. ground beef, browned and
  drained
10-3/4 oz. can tomato soup
1 c. salsa
1/2 c. milk
8-1/2 oz. can peas & carrots,
  drained
7 6-inch corn tortillas, cut into
  1-inch squares
1-1/2 t. chili powder
1 c. shredded Cheddar cheese,
  divided

61

Combine all ingredients except
1/2 cup cheese; spread in a 2-quart
casserole dish sprayed with non-stick
vegetable spray. Cover and bake at
400 degrees for 30 minutes, or until
hot. Sprinkle with remaining cheese;
let stand until cheese melts. Makes
4 servings.

Kathy Goscha
Topeka, KS
A south-of-the border dish
with a country twist!

Baked Pork Medallions

1/2 c. grated Parmesan cheese
.6-oz. pkg. Italian salad dressing
  mix
1/4 c. red wine vinegar
2 T. olive oil
2 lbs. pork tenderloin, sliced into
  1-inch-thick medallions
cooked fettuccine pasta
Garnish: chopped fresh chives

In a bowl, combine Parmesan cheese and salad dressing mix. In a separate bowl, whisk vinegar and oil. Dip medallions into vinegar mixture, then into Parmesan mixture. Place in an ungreased 13"x9" baking pan. Bake, uncovered, at 375 degrees for 30 to 35 minutes, until cooked through. Serve over pasta and garnish with chives. Serves 6 to 8.

Claire Bertram
Lexington, KY

My mother-in-law makes these fantastic medallions every New Year's Day. One more reason to celebrate!

Speedy Steak & Veggies

juice of 1 lime
salt and pepper to taste
1-1/2 lb. beef flank steak
1/2 bunch broccoli, cut into
    flowerets
2 c. baby carrots, sliced
2 ears corn, husked and cut into
    2-inch pieces
1 red onion, sliced into wedges
2 T. olive oil

Combine lime juice, salt and
pepper; brush over both sides of
beef. Place on a broiler pan and
broil, 5 minutes per side, turning
once. Set aside on a cutting board;
keep warm. Toss broccoli, carrots,
corn and onion with oil. Spoon onto
a lightly greased baking sheet in a
single layer. Bake at 475 degrees,
turning once, until tender, about
10 minutes. Slice steak into thin
strips on the diagonal and arrange on
a platter. Surround with vegetables.
Serves 4 to 6.

63

Jo Ann
A summertime favorite. We
find outstanding sweet corn
at our local farmers' market!

Little Meatloaves

1 egg, lightly beaten
1 c. pasta sauce, divided
1/2 c. dry bread crumbs
1/4 t. salt
1/4 c. fresh basil, coarsely chopped
   and divided
1 lb. ground beef
1 c. shredded mozzarella cheese

In a bowl, combine egg, 1/2 cup pasta sauce, bread crumbs, salt and half the basil. Add beef and 1/2 cup cheese; mix well. Shape into 4, 5-1/2 by 2-inch ovals. Place in a lightly greased 13"x9" baking pan. Spoon remaining sauce over top and sprinkle with remaining cheese. Bake, uncovered, at 450 degrees for 15 minutes. Sprinkle with remaining basil. Serves 4.

Tara Horton
Delaware, OH
Italian-style meatloaf for a family of four in less than half an hour? Oh, yes!

Jax's Cheeseburger Pizzas

1 lb. ground turkey
1/2 c. onion, diced
1/2 t. garlic salt
1/2 t. pepper
2 12-inch Italian pizza crusts
catsup and mustard to taste
16-oz. jar sliced bread & butter
    pickles, drained
8-oz. pkg. shredded Cheddar
    cheese

65

In a skillet over medium heat, brown turkey and onion; sprinkle with garlic salt and pepper. Drain and set aside. Place pizza crusts on ungreased baking sheets. Swirl catsup onto crusts, as you would do on a hamburger bun. Swirl mustard on top of the catsup (no need to smooth out or mix together). Divide turkey mixture evenly between the 2 crusts; arrange pickles on top of turkey. Sprinkle evenly with cheese. Bake at 425 degrees for 12 to 15 minutes, until cheese has melted. Cut into wedges to serve. Makes 2 pizzas, 8 servings each.

Jackie Daunce
Lockport, NY

This is a fast and easy supper I whip up for my husband and two boys. There are never any leftovers!

Mexicana Veggie Bake

1/2 c. green pepper, finely chopped
1/2 c. carrot, peeled and finely chopped
1/2 c. celery, finely chopped
1/2 c. onion, finely chopped
2 c. cooked rice
16-oz. can refried beans
15-oz. can black beans, drained and rinsed
1 c. salsa
12-oz. pkg. shredded Cheddar cheese, divided

Sauté vegetables in a lightly greased skillet over medium heat for 5 minutes, or until tender. Remove vegetables to a large bowl; add remaining ingredients except cheese. Layer half of mixture in a lightly greased 13"x9" baking pan; sprinkle with half the cheese. Repeat layering, ending with cheese. Bake, uncovered, at 350 degrees until heated through, about 15 to 20 minutes. Serves 6.

Tawnia Hultink
Ontario, Canada

Go meatless with layers of tasty sautéed vegetables and melted cheese.

Patsy's Stuffed Pork Chops

2 6-oz. pkgs. stuffing mix
8 boneless pork chops
2 T. oil
3 cloves garlic, sliced
salt and pepper to taste
2 c. applesauce
cinnamon to taste

Prepare stuffing mixes according to package instructions; set aside. Slicing horizontally into the sides, cut a pocket into the center of each pork chop. Evenly stuff chops with prepared stuffing. Drizzle oil and sprinkle garlic in a 13"x9" baking pan. Arrange chops in pan and season with salt and pepper. Top each chop with 1/4 cup applesauce and sprinkle with cinnamon. Bake, uncovered, at 425 degrees for 30 minutes, or until chops are no longer pink. Makes 8 servings.

67

Patricia Flaherty
Bergenfield, NJ

Prepare for raves and recipe requests when you serve these tasty chops!

Potluck Beef Sandwiches

1 lb. ground beef
1/4 onion, chopped
salt and pepper to taste
2/3 c. barbecue sauce
2 8-oz. tubes refrigerated
   crescent rolls
1/2 to 1 c. shredded Cheddar
   cheese
Garnish: additional barbecue
   sauce

In a skillet over medium heat, brown beef and onion. Add a little salt and pepper; drain. Mix in barbecue sauce. Place crescent rolls on a baking sheet and make a rectangle, pinching seams together. Spoon beef mixture down center of dough and sprinkle with cheese. Fold the sides over and seal dough down the center. Bake at 375 degrees for 20 minutes, or until golden. Slice into portions and serve with additional barbecue sauce. Serves 4.

Carmen Chandler
Roseburg, OR

I tried this recipe when I was first married, almost thirty years ago. I didn't know how to cook and this one turned out well every time!

Honey Cornmeal Chicken

1/2 c. honey, divided
4 boneless, skinless chicken
   breasts
1/4 c. yellow cornmeal
1/2 t. orange zest

Spray an 11"x7" baking pan with non-stick vegetable spray. Drizzle about 2 tablespoons honey onto the bottom of the pan; spread to lightly cover. Arrange chicken in dish and spread remaining honey over top. Mix together cornmeal and orange zest; sprinkle evenly over chicken. Cover and bake at 350 degrees for 15 minutes. Remove pan from oven. Uncover and spray tops of chicken with non-stick vegetable spray. Return to oven and bake, uncovered, for an additional 30 minutes, or until juices run clear when pierced. Serves 4.

69

Bonnie Hudson
Clearfield, PA

A four-ingredient recipe that tastes like a five-star winner!

Corn Surprise

15-1/4 oz. can corn
8-oz. pkg. small pasta shells,
   uncooked
16-oz. can cream-style corn
8-oz. pkg. shredded
   Mexican-blend cheese

Combine undrained corn and
remaining ingredients in a bowl.
Transfer to a greased 13"x9" baking
pan. Bake, covered, at 350 degrees for
45 minutes, or until pasta is tender.
As it bakes, stir casserole several times;
uncover for the last 10 minutes of
cooking. Serves 6 to 8.

Eva Rae Walters
Paola, KS

A winter warm-up recipe
that's easy to double,
making it perfect for
potlucks.

Tangy Watermelon Salad

14 c. watermelon, cubed
1 red onion, halved and thinly
   sliced
1 c. green onions, chopped
3/4 c. orange juice
5 T. red wine vinegar
2 T. plus 1-1/2 t. honey
1 T. green pepper, finely
   chopped
1/2 t. salt
1/4 t. pepper
1/4 t. garlic powder
1/4 t. onion powder
1/4 t. dry mustard
3/4 c. oil

In a large bowl, combine watermelon
and onion; set aside. In a small bowl,
combine orange juice, vinegar,
honey, green pepper and seasonings;
slowly whisk in oil. Pour over
watermelon mixture; toss gently.
Cover and refrigerate for at least
2 hours. Serve with a slotted spoon.
Makes about 10 servings.

Belva Conner
Hillsdale, IN

I won first prize for this
recipe at our county fair.
Everyone is surprised to
see watermelon and onions
together, but they always
ask for the recipe!

71

Ripe Tomato Tart

9-inch pie crust
1-1/2 c. shredded mozzarella
  cheese, divided
4 roma tomatoes, cut into wedges
3/4 c. fresh basil, chopped
4 cloves garlic, minced
1/2 c. mayonnaise
1/2 c. grated Parmesan cheese
1/8 t. white pepper

Line an ungreased 9" tart pan with pie crust; press crust into fluted sides of pan and trim edges. Bake at 450 degrees for 5 to 7 minutes; remove from oven. Sprinkle with 1/2 cup mozzarella cheese; let cool on a wire rack. Combine remaining ingredients; mix well and fill crust. Reduce heat to 375 degrees; bake for about 20 minutes, or until bubbly on top. Makes 6 servings.

Darlene Lohrman
Chicago, IL

Fresh roma tomatoes are available year 'round so you can enjoy this summery-tasting pie anytime.

Raspberry Spinach Salad

6-oz. pkg. baby spinach
1 pt. raspberries
1 c. pecan pieces
1/4 c. red onion, finely chopped
2 kiwis, peeled and cubed
1/2 c. raspberry vinaigrette salad
    dressing

In a large bowl, toss together all
ingredients. Serve immediately.
Serves 4.

73

Laina Lamb
Marion, OH

I've never met anyone who
didn't love this salad.
Excellent for picnics...just
toss when you get there!

Pamela's Garlic Bread

8-oz. pkg. cream cheese, softened
4-oz. can chopped black olives,
    drained
4 green onions, chopped
2 to 3 cloves garlic, finely chopped
1/4 c. Italian seasoning
1/4 c. butter, softened
1 loaf French bread, halved
    lengthwise

In a bowl, combine all ingredients
except bread; mix until well blended.
Evenly spread mixture on bread halves.
Place on an ungreased baking sheet.
Bake at 350 degrees for 10 to
15 minutes. Let cool and slice.
Makes 12 servings.

Pamela Delacruz
Mount Vernon, WA

People hover around the
kitchen waiting for this to
come out of the oven! You
can also use store-bought
garlic bread...just omit
the garlic and butter.

Fried Spaghetti

12-oz. pkg. thin spaghetti,
   uncooked
3 T. sesame oil
1/2 onion, chopped
1/4 c. frozen peas
1/4 c. bacon bits
2 T. soy sauce
2 T. teriyaki sauce

Cook spaghetti according to package directions; drain. Meanwhile, in a large saucepan, heat oil over medium heat. Sauté onion, frozen peas and bacon bits for 3 minutes, or until onion is soft. Stir in soy sauce, teriyaki sauce and spaghetti. Mix everything well. Cook for 5 minutes, stirring occasionally. Serves 4.

75

Tiffany Jones
Locust Grove, AR

My dad and I love Chinese food. I tried spaghetti noodles instead of rice...it turned out to be a favorite!

Sour Cream Cornbread

1-1/2 c. self-rising cornmeal
2 T. self-rising flour
1/4 c. sugar
2 eggs, beaten
1-1/2 c. sour cream
2/3 c. oil
1/2 c. buttermilk

Combine all ingredients in a large bowl and mix well. Pour into a greased 9"x9" baking pan. Bake at 350 degrees for 25 to 30 minutes, until golden. Makes 9 servings.

Dueley Lucas
Somerset, KY

This is the most-requested bread at all of our church dinners!

Spiced Baked Fruit

16-oz. can apricot halves,
   drained
16-oz. can pear halves, drained
29-oz. can peach halves, drained
8-oz. can pineapple slices,
   drained and 1/2 c. juice
   reserved
1/3 c. brown sugar, packed
1 T. butter
1/2 t. cinnamon
1/4 t. ground cloves

77

In a greased 13"x9" baking pan,
starting at the short end, arrange
rows of fruit in the following order:
half the apricots, half the pears and
half the peaches. Repeat rows.
Arrange pineapple over fruit. In a
saucepan over medium heat, combine
reserved pineapple juice and
remaining ingredients. Cook and
stir until sugar is dissolved and butter
is melted. Pour over fruit. Bake,
uncovered, at 350 degrees for 20 to
25 minutes, until heated through.
Serves 6 to 8.

Regina Ferrigno
Gooseberry Patch

Guests "ooh" and "ahh"
when they discover the
rows of fruit under the
pineapple...so pretty!

Spicy Carrot French Fries

2 lbs. carrots, peeled and cut into
   matchsticks
4 T. olive oil, divided
1 T. seasoned salt
2 t. ground cumin
1 t. chili powder
1 t. pepper
Garnish: ranch salad dressing

Place carrots in a plastic zipping bag.
Sprinkle with 3 tablespoons oil and
seasonings; toss to coat. Drizzle
remaining oil over a baking sheet; place
carrots in a single layer on sheet. Bake,
uncovered, at 425 degrees for 25 to
35 minutes, until carrots are golden.
Serve with salad dressing for dipping.
Makes 4 to 6 servings.

Kelly Gray
Weston, WV

My children didn't know until
they were almost grown that
this dish was good for them!
The sweet flavor mixed with
the spicy seasonings is
unusual and delicious.

BBQ Beef & Wagon Wheels Salad

2 c. cooked wagon wheel pasta
1 c. deli roast beef, cut in thin
   strips
3/4 c. onion, sliced
1/2 c. green pepper, chopped
2/3 c. barbecue sauce
2 T. Dijon mustard
2 c. red leaf lettuce, torn
2 c. green leaf lettuce, torn
Garnish: 1 tomato, sliced

Rinse pasta with cold water; drain
well. Combine pasta, beef, onion
and green pepper in a medium
bowl; set aside. In a small bowl, mix
together barbecue sauce and mustard;
stir into beef mixture. Chill. At
serving time, toss together red and
green lettuce; arrange on salad plates.
Spoon beef mixture over lettuce;
garnish with tomato slices. Serves 4.

79

Vickie

A hearty salad for
cowboy-size appetites.

French Onion Biscuits

8-oz. container French onion dip
1/4 c. milk
1 t. dried parsley
2 c. biscuit baking mix
1 T. butter, melted

In a large bowl, whisk together onion dip, milk and parsley until smooth. Stir in baking mix until well blended. Drop dough by spoonfuls onto a lightly greased baking sheet, making 12 biscuits. Bake at 450 degrees for 7 to 8 minutes, until lightly golden. Immediately brush tops of biscuits with melted butter. Makes one dozen.

Lane Ann Miller
Trenton, KY

These biscuits are quick, easy and scrumptious...wonderful with soups or Italian dishes.

Company Green Beans

3 slices bacon, crisply cooked,
    crumbled and 1 T. drippings
    reserved
2 t. garlic, minced
1/4 c. red onion, finely grated
2 14-1/2 oz. cans French-style
    green beans, drained
1 tomato, chopped
salt and pepper to taste
1/2 c. shredded sharp Cheddar
    cheese

In a skillet over medium heat, sauté garlic and onion in reserved bacon drippings until slightly softened. Remove from heat and stir in green beans, tomato and seasonings to taste. Place in a greased 8"x8" baking pan and sprinkle with cheese. Bake, covered, at 400 degrees for 15 minutes. Uncover, reduce heat to 350 degrees and bake an additional 15 minutes. Serves 4 to 6.

81

Stephanie Norton
Saginaw, TX

My husband's family has been sharing this dish at gatherings for generations. It's a staple at our house as well, even for those who don't like vegetables!

Chili Rice

3 c. cooked rice
10-3/4 oz. can cream of celery
   soup
4-oz. can diced green chiles,
   or to taste
1 c. shredded Monterey Jack cheese
1 c. sour cream
Optional: dried chives

Combine all ingredients except chives.
Transfer to a lightly greased 2-quart
casserole dish. Bake, uncovered, at
350 degrees for 20 minutes. Garnish
with chives, if desired. Serves 6 to 8.

Sally Davison
Page, AZ

People love this
five-ingredient casserole!
It goes well with other
southwestern dishes.

Black-Eyed Pea Salad

1/3 c. onion, grated
1/3 c. fresh parsley, minced
3 T. cider vinegar
2 T. oil
1 clove garlic, minced
1/4 t. salt
2 16-oz. cans black-eyed peas,
  drained
1 tomato, diced
1 head lettuce, shredded
Garnish: tomato wedges,
  green pepper rings

83

Combine onion, parsley, vinegar,
oil, garlic and salt in a large bowl.
Add peas and tomato; chill. At
serving time, arrange lettuce on a
platter. Spoon mixture over lettuce.
Garnish with tomato wedges and
green pepper rings. Serves 6 to 8.

Annette Sykes
Springfield, TN

My friends & family always
ask me to bring this unique
salad to potluck suppers.

Sweet-and-Sour Slaw

3-oz. pkg. chicken-flavored
   ramen noodles, uncooked
16-oz. pkg. shredded coleslaw mix
1 c. slivered almonds
1 c. sunflower kernels
4 green onions, chopped
6-oz. pkg. grilled chicken breast
   strips
11-oz. can mandarin oranges,
   drained

Break ramen noodles into pieces; set aside seasoning packet for dressing. In a large bowl, toss noodles with remaining ingredients. Drizzle with Dressing; toss again. Cover and refrigerate for at least one hour. Toss again before serving. Serves 6.

Dressing:

1/4 to 1/2 c. olive oil
1/4 c. sugar
3 T. white vinegar
reserved seasoning packet

Whisk together all ingredients.

Vicki Sebring
Mentor, OH

A different take on coleslaw that could be a meal in itself!

Hawaiian Asparagus

1 lb. asparagus, trimmed and cut
   in 1-inch diagonal slices
2 T. olive oil
1/4 c. beef broth
4 to 5 slices bacon, crisply
   cooked and cut into bite-size
   pieces
pepper to taste
2 T. sesame seed, lightly toasted

In a skillet over medium heat, cook
asparagus in oil for 2 to 3 minutes.
Add beef broth; cover, reduce heat
and simmer for 4 to 5 minutes,
until asparagus is cooked to desired
tenderness. Stir in bacon, pepper
and sesame seed. Serves 4.

85

Beth Brown
Trent Woods, NC

This recipe was given to
my mom forty years ago by
another military wife when
my Air Force family was
stationed in Japan. We make
this when asparagus is
in season.

Mustard-Topped Cauliflower

1 head cauliflower, cut into
   flowerets
1/3 c. water
1/2 c. mayonnaise
1 T. onion, finely chopped
2 t. mustard
1/4 t. salt
2/3 c. shredded Cheddar cheese
1/4 t. paprika

Place cauliflower in a deep microwave-safe casserole dish; add water. Cover and microwave on high for about 12 minutes, or until cauliflower is tender; drain. In a bowl, combine mayonnaise, onion, mustard and salt. Spoon mayonnaise mixture over cauliflower; sprinkle with cheese and paprika. Microwave, uncovered, for 2 minutes, or until cheese is melted. Serves 4 to 6.

Sandra Moy
Clarendon, NY

This recipe is amazing. It takes only a few minutes and you have a hearty side dish that goes so well with baked ham.

Baked Spinach & Rice

10-oz. pkg. frozen chopped
    spinach, thawed and well
    drained
2 c. cooked rice
8-oz. pkg. pasteurized process
    cheese spread, cubed
1/3 c. onion, chopped
1/3 c. red pepper, chopped
3 eggs, beaten
1/8 t. pepper
Optional: 1/4 lb. turkey bacon,
    crisply cooked and crumbled

In a large bowl, combine all
ingredients, mixing well. Spread in
a greased 10"x6" baking pan; smooth
top with a spatula. Bake, uncovered,
at 350 degrees for 30 minutes. Let
stand 5 minutes; cut into squares.
Makes 8 servings.

87

Elena Smith
Monterey, CA
I find this casserole is just
as tasty if I substitute
four egg whites for the
whole eggs and use a
"light" cheese spread.

Slow-Cooker Potatoes Dijonnaise

1/3 c. Dijon mustard
1/2 c. olive oil
1/3 c. red wine vinegar
salt and pepper to taste
6 potatoes, cubed
1 onion, chopped

Blend mustard, oil and vinegar in a medium bowl; add salt and pepper to taste. Add potatoes and onion, stirring to coat. Transfer to a slow cooker; cover and cook on low setting for 8 to 10 hours, until potatoes are tender. Makes 4 to 5 servings.

Dawn Dhooghe
Concord, NC

The house smells heavenly while this is cooking!

Garden Rice Salad

2 c. long-cooking brown rice,
   uncooked
1 carrot, peeled and sliced
1/2 cucumber, chopped
1/2 onion, chopped
1 green pepper, chopped
8 radishes, sliced
2 stalks celery, sliced
11-oz. can corn, drained and
   rinsed

89

Cook rice according to package
instructions; fluff with a fork and
let cool. In a bowl, combine rice
and remaining ingredients. Drizzle
with Dijon Dressing and toss to
coat. Serves 4.

Dijon Dressing:

2 T. white vinegar
1 T. olive oil
1/4 c. lemon juice
2 T. Dijon mustard
salt and pepper to taste

Whisk together all ingredients in
order listed.

Lori Peterson
Effingham, KS
Serve this deliciously
different salad in a clear
glass bowl to show off
all the colors!

Orange-Filled Napoleons

8-oz. pkg. frozen puff pastry
   sheets, thawed
2 c. vanilla ice cream, softened
1 orange, peeled and thinly sliced
Garnish: powdered sugar

Unfold pastry and cut into 8 rectangles.
Place on an ungreased baking sheet and
bake at 375 degrees for 20 minutes, or
until puffed and golden. Let cool. To
serve, split pastries lengthwise. Spoon
ice cream on one half; top evenly with
orange slices and replace pastry top.
Dust with powdered sugar. Makes
4 servings.

Vickie

A snap to make and
elegant to serve!

Strawberry Dessert

16-1/2 oz. tube refrigerated sugar cookie dough
8-oz. pkg. cream cheese, softened
8-oz. container frozen whipped topping, thawed and divided
1 qt. strawberries, hulled and sliced
13-1/2 oz. container strawberry glaze

Slice cookie dough and press into the bottom of an ungreased 13"x9" baking pan. Bake at 350 degrees for 13 to 16 minutes, until lightly golden. Cool completely on a wire rack. Mix cream cheese and one cup whipped topping. Spread over cookie crust. Stir strawberries and glaze together and spread over top. Cover and chill. Cut into squares and serve with remaining whipped topping. Serves 10 to 12.

91

Janice Nichols
North Manchester, IN

A lady where I worked would surprise the department with this delicious dessert. The sight of those fresh, red strawberries would make your mouth water!

Joyce's Chocolate Chip Pie

2 eggs, beaten
1/4 c. all-purpose flour
1/3 c. sugar
1-1/2 c. brown sugar, packed
1 c. chopped pecans
1/2 c. butter, melted and cooled
    slightly
3/4 c. mini semi-sweet chocolate
    chips
9-inch pie crust
Optional: whipped cream,
    additional mini chocolate chips

In a bowl, mix eggs, flour, sugars, pecans and melted butter until well blended. Sprinkle chocolate chips in unbaked pie crust. Pour egg mixture over top. Bake at 350 degrees for 45 to 50 minutes, until golden. Pie will become firm as it cools. Garnish as desired. Serves 8.

Joyce Timko
Granite City, IL

Chocolate, butter and
whipped cream...oh, my!

Bananas Foster

1/2 c. butter, melted
1/4 c. brown sugar, packed
6 bananas, cut into 1-inch slices
1/4 c. rum or 1/4 t. rum extract
Garnish: vanilla ice cream

Stir together butter, brown sugar, bananas and rum or extract in a slow cooker. Cover and cook on low setting for one hour. Use a slotted spoon to place bananas into serving dishes. Top with a scoop of ice cream and drizzle with sauce from the slow cooker. Makes 4 servings.

93

Jo Ann
Guests will flip over this decadent slow-cooker dessert!

Peanut Butter Surprise Cookies

16-1/2 oz. tube refrigerated peanut
   butter cookie dough
12 mini peanut butter cups
1/3 c. semi-sweet chocolate chips
1 t. shortening

Divide cookie dough into 12 pieces.
With floured fingers, wrap one piece of
dough around each peanut butter cup.
Place on ungreased baking sheets. Bake
at 350 degrees for 10 to 15 minutes,
until golden. Cool on baking sheets
one minute; remove to wire rack to
cool completely. In a saucepan, melt
chocolate chips and shortening over
low heat, stirring constantly. Drizzle
melted chocolate over cookies. Let
stand until set. Makes one dozen.

Sherry Gordon
Arlington Heights, IL
Yum, yum, yum! I like to
divvy up the dough between
baking sheets and chill
the second batch while the
first is baking.

Chocolate-Berry Trifles

1 pt. blueberries, divided
1 pt. strawberries, hulled and
    sliced
1 angel food cake, cubed
1 c. chocolate syrup
12-oz. container frozen whipped
    topping, thawed

In a bowl, crush 1/4 cup blueberries.
Stir in remaining blueberries and
strawberries. Place several cake cubes
in the bottom of 10 clear serving
cups or bowls. Top with a layer of
berry mixture. Drizzle lightly with
chocolate syrup, then top with a
layer of whipped topping. Repeat
layers until each cup is full, ending
with a layer of whipped topping and
a light drizzle of chocolate syrup.
Makes 10 servings.

95

Melody Taynor
Everett, WA

I've made all kinds of
trifles, but this is my
first one with chocolate.
My sister says it's
my best yet!

Quick & Easy Nutty Cheese Bars

18-1/2 oz. pkg. golden butter
  cake mix
1-1/2 c. chopped pecans or
  walnuts, divided
3/4 c. butter, melted
2 8-oz. pkgs. cream cheese,
  softened
1 c. brown sugar, packed

In a bowl, combine dry cake mix,
3/4 cup pecans and melted butter; stir
until well blended. Press mixture into
the bottom of a greased 13"x9" baking
pan. Combine cream cheese and brown
sugar in a separate bowl. Stir until well
mixed. Spread evenly over crust.
Sprinkle with remaining pecans. Bake
at 350 degrees for 25 to 30 minutes,
until edges are golden and cheese
topping is set. Cool completely in pan
on wire rack. Cut into bars. Refrigerate
leftovers. Makes 2 dozen.

Donnie Carter
Wellington, TX
This recipe is now the
requested birthday gift of
family & friends. They're
so good cold!

Apple Crisp Pie

21-oz. can apple pie filling
9-inch deep-dish pie crust
1/2 c. brown sugar, packed
1/2 c. sugar
1 c. quick-cooking oats,
   uncooked
1 T. cinnamon
1/4 c. butter, sliced

Pour apple pie filling into pie crust. In a separate bowl, combine sugars, oats and cinnamon. Sprinkle over top; dot with butter. Bake at 375 degrees for 30 minutes. Serves 8.

97

Cris Hamilton
Anna, TX

My sister-in-law made this for us one Easter. I can't believe how easy and delicious it is!

Mariachi Margarita Dip

8-oz. pkg. cream cheese, softened
1/3 c. frozen margarita drink mix,
   thawed
2 T. orange juice
1/4 c. powdered sugar
1/2 c. whipped cream
Garnish: corn syrup, colored sugar
assorted fruit slices and cubes

In a bowl, beat together cream cheese,
margarita mix, orange juice and
powdered sugar until smooth. Fold
whipped cream into mixture until well
blended. Cover and chill one hour.
Dip rim of serving bowl in corn syrup.
Shake off excess and dip rim in colored
sugar. Spoon dip into bowl and serve
with fruit. Serves 6 to 8.

Lynda Robson
Boston, MA

Turn any gathering into a
fiesta when you serve this
appetizer-style dessert!

Mom's Chocolate Malt Shoppe Pie

1-oz. pkg. sugar-free white
   chocolate instant pudding mix
4 to 5 t. chocolate malt powder
1 c. milk
8-oz. container frozen whipped
   topping, thawed and divided
1-1/2 c. malted milk balls,
   crushed and divided
9-inch chocolate cookie crust

In a bowl, mix together dry pudding
mix, malt powder and milk. Fold in
3/4 of the whipped topping and
1-1/4 cups crushed candy; spread
in crust. Spread with remaining
whipped topping. Sprinkle with
remaining candy; chill until set.
Serves 8.

99

Nancy Brush
Robinson, IL
We're a family of chocoholics
and also love chocolate
malts, so my mom created this
pie that combines our two
favorite things.

Root Beer Float Cake

18-1/2 oz. pkg. white cake mix
2-1/4 c. root beer, chilled and
    divided
1/4 c. oil
2 eggs, beaten
1 env. whipped topping mix

In a large bowl, combine dry cake mix,
1-1/4 cups root beer, oil and eggs; beat
until well blended. Pour into a greased
13"x9" baking pan. Bake at 350 degrees
for 30 to 35 minutes; cool completely.
In a medium bowl, with an electric
mixer on high speed, beat whipped
topping mix and remaining root beer
until soft peaks form; frost cake. Makes
24 servings.

Mary Patenaude
Griswold, CT

This cake is so easy
to make. And it tastes
just like a root beer float!

Coconut Cupcakes

2/3 c. sweetened flaked coconut
1-1/4 c. powdered sugar
1-1/2 c. all-purpose flour
1/8 t. salt
1 t. baking powder
1/2 c. butter, melted and cooled
    slightly
5 egg whites, beaten
12 raspberries

In a bowl, combine coconut, powdered sugar, flour, salt and baking powder. Mix in melted butter. Stir in egg whites until well combined. Line a muffin tin with 12 paper liners; fill liners with batter 2/3 full. Bake at 375 degrees for 12 to 15 minutes, until firm. Let cool. Spread Vanilla Frosting onto cupcakes; top each with a raspberry and let set. Makes one dozen.

Vanilla Frosting:

1-1/2 c. powdered sugar
1 t. vanilla extract
4 to 5 t. hot water

In a bowl, combine all ingredients. Beat to desired consistency, adding more water or sugar as needed.

101

Barb Horton
Cincinnati, OH

Fresh raspberries are perfect little toppers for these wonderful cupcakes!

Mix-and-Go Chocolate Cookies

18-1/2 oz. pkg. chocolate cake mix
1/2 c. butter, softened
2 eggs, beaten
1 c. white chocolate chips

In a bowl, combine dry cake mix, butter and eggs until smooth. Mix in chocolate chips. Drop by tablespoonfuls onto ungreased baking sheets. Bake at 350 degrees for 8 to 10 minutes. Let cool on baking sheet for 5 minutes; remove to wire rack to cool completely. Makes about 2 dozen.

Rhonda Reeder
Ellicott City, MD

Just as decadent with peanut butter or milk chocolate chips!

Oh-So-Easy Fruit Tartlets

2 3.4-oz. pkgs. instant vanilla
   pudding mix
3-1/2 c. milk
2 t. lemon zest
2 4-oz. pkgs. mini graham
   cracker crusts
Garnish: sliced kiwi, peaches
   or strawberries, mandarin
   oranges, raspberries,
   blueberries
1/2 c. apple jelly, melted

103

Prepare pudding according to
package directions, using the milk.
Stir in lemon zest. Spoon into
mini crusts; arrange fruit on top as
desired. Use a pastry brush to glaze
fruit with melted jelly. Set tartlets
on a baking sheet, cover and chill.
Makes one dozen.

Jennifer Licon-Conner
Gooseberry Patch

Guests will be so impressed
with these bakery-style
tarts! Use your favorite
pudding flavor and fruit to
make different varieties.

Fudge Cobbler

1/2 c. butter
1-oz. sq. unsweetened baking
 chocolate
1 c. sugar
1/2 c. all-purpose flour
1 t. vanilla extract
2 eggs, beaten
Optional: vanilla ice cream

Melt butter and chocolate in a saucepan over low heat, stirring often. Remove from heat; stir in sugar, flour, vanilla and eggs. Pour batter into a greased 8"x8" baking pan; bake at 325 degrees for 20 to 22 minutes. Serve warm with ice cream, if desired. Serves 9.

Sandy Bernards
Valencia, CA

Mmm...so easy, so luscious.
What could be better?

White Chocolate-Butterscotch Pretzels

1 lb. white melting chocolate
15-oz. pkg. mini pretzels
1/2 c. butterscotch chips

Break up white chocolate into about 6 pieces and place in a microwave-safe dish. Microwave on high for 1-1/2 to 2 minutes, stirring every 30 seconds, until melted and smooth. Dip pretzels into the chocolate and lay on wax paper to dry. Melt butterscotch chips in the microwave repeating instructions for the chocolate. Spoon melted butterscotch into a plastic zipping bag; snip off a corner. Drizzle butterscotch over pretzels. Let pretzels set for a few hours, or overnight if packing into gift bags. Makes about 2 pounds.

105

Buffy VanSickle
Buhl, ID

Kids love to help with this simple-to-make treat! Perfect for Halloween treat bags or Christmas goodie trays.

Oh, Harry! Bars

3/4 c. butter, softened
1 c. dark brown sugar, packed
1/2 c. honey
1/2 t. ground ginger
4 c. quick-cooking oats, uncooked
6-oz. pkg. milk chocolate chips
2/3 c. creamy peanut butter

In a bowl, beat butter and brown sugar until light and fluffy. Beat in honey and ginger; stir in oats. With moistened hands, pat mixture into the bottom of a greased 13"x9" baking pan. Bake at 350 degrees until bubbly and lightly golden, about 25 minutes. In a microwave-safe bowl, heat chocolate chips and peanut butter on high for one minute. Stir; heat for another minute. Stir until all chips are melted. Spread chocolate mixture over bars and refrigerate until set. Cut into bars. Makes 2 dozen.

Valarie Lewis
Clifford Township, PA

My mother handed down this dessert recipe to me. Growing up, it was a favorite among us kids!

Little Cheesecakes

1 c. graham cracker crumbs
1 c. sugar, divided
1/4 c. butter, melted
2 8-oz. pkgs. cream cheese,
　softened
2 eggs, beaten
1 t. vanilla extract
14-1/2 oz. can cherry pie filling

Place mini paper liners into 24 mini muffin cups. In a bowl, combine cracker crumbs, 1/4 cup sugar and butter. Press about 2 teaspoons of mixture into the bottom of each liner. In a bowl, beat cream cheese and remaining sugar together. Add eggs and vanilla; mix well. Evenly spoon cheese mixture over crusts. Bake at 350 degrees for 15 minutes, or until set. Cool. Top with cherry pie filling. Makes 2 dozen.

107

Nina Jones
Springfield, OH

I started making this recipe when I was a teenager...now it's a favorite of my teenage son and his friends.

Easy Apple Popovers

16.2-oz. tube refrigerated flaky
   biscuits
1/2 c. sweetened applesauce
2 to 4 T. milk
1 c. powdered sugar

Spray a muffin tin with non-stick
vegetable spray. Separate biscuits. Press
a biscuit into the bottom and partway
up the sides of each muffin cup. Spoon
applesauce into biscuits. Bake at
400 degrees for 10 to 15 minutes, until
biscuits are done. Remove popovers
from muffin tin; let cool. In a bowl,
add milk to powdered sugar, a
tablespoon at a time, until mixture
is a drizzling consistency. Drizzle glaze
over popovers. Makes 8 servings.

Debra Coogle
Oglethorpe, GA
These fruity treats are
delish! I made up this recipe
when I needed a dessert to
carry to the family of a
friend who had just come
home from the hospital.

Raspberry Cheese Ball

2 8-oz pkgs. cream cheese,
   softened
1/4 c. raspberry preserves
2 c. pecans, finely chopped and
   divided
assorted cookies and crackers

In a bowl, beat cream cheese until
creamy; mix in preserves and one cup
pecans. Shape into a ball and roll in
remaining pecans. Serve with cookies
and crackers. Serves 6 to 8.

109

Julie Ann Perkins
Anderson, IN

Try different preserves
to accommodate everyone's
tastes...cherry, apricot
or even boysenberry!

Hawaiian Kielbasa, page 117

Ham & Ranch Potatoes, page 157

Tami's Taco Soup, page 167

Mom's Blueberry Cobbler, page 162

101 *Slow-Cooker* RECIPES

Apple Brown Betty, page 193

Zesty Macaroni & Cheese, page 188

Midwest Chicken Sandwich, page 125

Slow-cooked, tried & true favorites that everyone's
sure to love…savory mains, simple sides,
simmering soups and tasty dessert treats!

Hearty Beef Stew, page 183

Anne's Chicken Burritos, page 191

Just Peachy Cider, page 136

Slow-Cooker TIPS

★ Spray the crock with non-stick vegetable spray before filling. Clean-up will be a snap!

★ For best results, fill the slow cooker about 1/2 to 3/4 full of ingredients.

★ Little or no added liquid is needed…just add what the recipe calls for. There's no evaporation, so all of the tasty juices stay right in the crock.

★ Don't peek! Cooking time can increase by 15 to 20 minutes every time the lid is lifted.

★ Toward the end of cooking time, taste and adjust seasonings. The flavor of herbs tends to grow milder with long cooking, so you may want to add a little more.

★ At high altitude, slow cooking will take a little longer. Add an extra 30 minutes of cooking time to each hour in a recipe.

Pintos & Pork Over Corn Chips

16-oz. pkg. dried pinto beans
3-lb. pork loin roast, trimmed
7 c. water
4-oz. can chopped green chiles
1/2 c. onion, chopped
2 cloves garlic, minced
2 T. chili powder
1 T. ground cumin
1 T. salt
1 t. dried oregano
Garnish: corn chips, sour cream,
   shredded Cheddar cheese,
   chopped tomatoes,
   shredded lettuce

113

Cover beans with water in a large
soup pot; soak overnight. Drain.
Add beans and remaining ingredients
except garnish to a slow cooker.
Cover and cook on low setting for
9 hours. Remove meat, discarding
bones; return to slow cooker. Cook,
uncovered, for 30 minutes, until
thickened. Serve over corn chips;
garnish as desired. Makes
10 servings.

Susan Butters
Bountiful, UT

A hearty dish that
feeds a crowd of hungry
people...easily!

Hot Buffalo Dip

3 to 4 boneless, skinless chicken
    breasts, cooked and chopped
1 c. hot wing sauce
2 8-oz. pkgs. cream cheese,
    cubed and softened
1/2 c. shredded Cheddar cheese
1/4 c. blue cheese salad dressing
corn chips, celery stalks

In a slow cooker, mix together all
ingredients except corn chips and
celery stalks. Cover and cook on low
setting for 3 to 4 hours. Serve with
corn chips and celery stalks for
dipping. Makes 8 to 10 servings.

Vickie

One of my favorite party
dips...oh-so easy to make
and we all love it!

Honey Sesame Wings

3 lbs. chicken wings
salt and pepper to taste
2 c. honey
1 c. soy sauce
1/2 c. catsup
1/4 c. oil
2 cloves garlic, minced
Garnish: sesame seed

Place chicken wings on an
ungreased broiler pan; sprinkle
with salt and pepper. Place pan
4 to 5 inches under broiler. Broil
for 10 minutes on each side, or
until chicken is golden. Transfer
wings to a slow cooker. Combine
remaining ingredients except sesame
seed; pour over wings. Cover and
cook on low setting for 4 to 5 hours,
or high setting for 2 to 2-1/2 hours.
Arrange on a serving platter; sprinkle
with sesame seed. Makes about
2-1/2 dozen.

Kimberly Hancock
Murrieta, CA

Always a hit with young &
old alike...these wings are
sweet and tangy, but not too
spicy. We just love 'em!

Tahitian Rice Pudding

3/4 c. long-cooking rice,
   uncooked
15-oz. can cream of coconut
12-oz. can evaporated milk
2-3/4 c. water
Optional: 1 T. dark rum
2/3 c. sweetened flaked coconut

In a slow cooker, stir rice, cream of coconut, evaporated milk and water until combined. Cover and cook on low setting for 4 to 5 hours. Remove crock from slow cooker. Stir in rum, if using. Let pudding cool for 10 minutes. Heat a small non-stick skillet over medium heat. Add coconut; cook and stir for 4 to 5 minutes, until toasted. Transfer coconut to a plate. Spoon pudding into dessert bowls; sprinkle with coconut. Makes 6 to 8 servings.

Beth Kramer
Port Saint Lucie, FL
Scrumptious served
warm or cold.

Hawaiian Kielbasa

3 lbs. Kielbasa, sliced into
   2-inch chunks
15-1/4 oz. can crushed pineapple
18-oz. bottle barbecue sauce
1/2 c. brown sugar, packed
1 T. ground ginger
1 t. onion powder
1 t. garlic powder

Combine all ingredients in a slow
cooker. Mix well. Cover and cook
on low setting for about 2 hours,
until warmed through, or on high
setting for about 30 minutes.
Makes 10 to 15 servings.

117

Aemelia Manier
West Branch, MI

A crowd pleaser. I have
learned to carry a copy of
the recipe with me whenever
I serve it, because people
are always asking for it!

Hot Broccoli-Cheese Dip

3/4 c. butter
3 stalks celery, thinly sliced
1 onion, chopped
4-oz. can sliced mushrooms,
     drained
3 T. all-purpose flour
10-3/4 oz. can cream of
     celery soup
3 c. shredded Cheddar cheese
10-oz. pkg. frozen chopped
     broccoli, thawed

Melt butter in a skillet over medium heat; sauté celery, onion and mushrooms. Stir in flour; mix well. Transfer mixture to a lightly greased slow cooker; mix in remaining ingredients. Cover and cook on high setting until cheese is melted, stirring every 15 minutes. Continue cooking, covered, on low setting for 2 to 4 hours. Makes 10 to 12 servings.

Rogene Rogers
Bemidji, MN

Be sure to serve this yummy dip with hearty crackers...you'll want to get every drop!

French Dip Sandwiches

3-lb. beef chuck roast,
  trimmed
2 c. water
1/2 c. soy sauce
1 t. dried rosemary
1 t. dried thyme
1 t. garlic powder
1 bay leaf
3 to 4 whole peppercorns
8 French rolls, split

Place roast in a slow cooker; add remaining ingredients except rolls. Cover and cook on high for 5 to 6 hours. Remove roast from broth; shred with 2 forks and keep warm. Discard bay leaf; serve beef on rolls. Makes 6 to 8 sandwiches.

119

Debbie DeValk
Springfield, TN
Serve the savory broth from the slow cooker in small cups for dipping.

Cajun Spiced Pecans

16-oz. pkg. pecan halves
1/4 c. butter, melted
1 T. chili powder
1 t. dried basil
1 t. dried oregano
1 t. dried thyme
1 t. salt
1/2 t. onion powder
1/4 t. garlic powder
1/4 t. cayenne pepper

Combine all ingredients in a slow cooker. Cover and cook on high setting for 15 minutes. Turn to low setting and cook, uncovered, for 2 hours, stirring occasionally. Transfer nuts to a baking sheet; cool completely. Store in an airtight container. Makes 12 to 16 servings.

Kerry Mayer
Dunham Springs, LA

Fill small ribbon-tied bags with these delightful nuts to send home with guests...they'll love it!

Aunt B's Sloppy Joes

3 lbs. ground turkey
1 c. onion, chopped
1 c. green pepper, chopped
2 cloves garlic, chopped
1-1/2 c. catsup
1/2 c. water
1/4 c. mustard
1/4 c. cider vinegar
1/4 c. Worcestershire sauce
1 T. chili powder
10 whole-wheat hamburger
   buns, split

121

In a skillet over medium heat, cook ground turkey, onion, pepper and garlic until browned and tender; drain. Combine in a slow cooker with remaining ingredients except buns. Cover and cook on low setting for 6 to 8 hours, or on high setting for 3 to 4 hours. Spoon onto buns. Makes 10 sandwiches.

**Bryna Dunlap
Muskogee, OK**

For a quick & easy meal, ladle leftovers over cooked rotini pasta.

Creamy Hot Corn Dip

2 8-oz. pkgs. cream cheese,
  softened
2 15-1/4 oz. cans corn, drained
1/2 c. butter
2 jalapeño peppers, diced
tortilla chips

Combine all ingredients except tortilla chips in a slow cooker. Cover and cook on high setting for 30 minutes; stir until smooth. Reduce setting to low to keep warm. The longer it cooks, the spicier it will get. Serve with tortilla chips. Makes 15 servings.

Tanya Miller
Millersburg, OH

My husband calls this dip "man food!" The last time I made this dip, people were eating it by the spoonful!

Pepperoncini Italian Beef Roast

4-lb. beef chuck roast
8-oz. jar pepperoncini peppers,
    drained and juice reserved
1 onion, sliced
2 1-oz. pkgs. au jus mix
8 to 10 hoagie rolls, split

Place roast in a slow cooker; pour
reserved pepper juice over top. Cover
and cook on low setting for 6 to
8 hours, until very tender. Remove
roast and shred with 2 forks; stir
back into juice in slow cooker. Add
peppers and onion. Blend au jus
mix with a little of the juice from
slow cooker until dissolved. Pour
over meat; add water if needed to
cover roast. Cover and cook for an
additional hour. Serve beef spooned
onto rolls. Makes 8 to 10 sandwiches.

123

Vickie
These sandwiches are zesty
and oh-so easy to fix!

Honeyed Fruit Juice

64-oz. bottle cranberry-apple
   juice cocktail
2 c. apple juice
1 c. pomegranate juice
1/2 c. orange juice
2/3 c. honey
3 4-inch cinnamon sticks
10 whole cloves
2 T. orange zest

Combine juices and honey in a
slow cooker. Wrap cinnamon sticks
and cloves in a double thickness of
cheesecloth; bring up corners of cloth
and tie with kitchen string to form a
bag. Add to slow cooker along with zest.
Cover and cook on low setting for one
to 2 hours. Discard spice bag before
serving. Makes 3 quarts.

Brenda Smith
Marysville, OH

Coming in from ice skating,
we were chilled to the
bone. Luckily Mom had this
wonderful juice blend
warming in the slow cooker!

Midwest Chicken Sandwich

50-oz. can dark and white
   boned chicken, drained
   and shredded
26-oz. can cream of chicken
   soup
salt and pepper to taste
24 sandwich buns, split
Optional: pickle slices

Mix chicken and soup in a slow
cooker. Cover and cook on low
setting for 3 to 4 hours. Add salt
and pepper to taste; stir well.
Spoon onto buns and garnish
with pickle slices, if desired.
Makes about 24 sandwiches.

125

Linda Ketcham
Columbus, OH

This is so quick & easy to
put together, it's a recipe
I can count on for every
large gathering.

Seaside Crab Dip

2 8-oz. pkgs. cream cheese
3 T. butter
1 bunch green onions, chopped
1 lb. crabmeat
onion and garlic salt to taste
garlic melba toast

In a microwave-safe bowl, mix all
ingredients together except melba
toast. Microwave on high setting until
warm. Pour into a slow cooker; cover
and keep warm on low setting. Serve
with melba toast. Makes 24 servings.

Lisa Columbo
Appleton, WI
This couldn't be easier
to whip up. The slow cooker
keeps it warm and creamy
until the party ends.

Chipotle Shredded Beef

2-1/2 lb. beef chuck roast,
  trimmed
14-oz. can diced tomatoes
7-oz. can chipotle sauce
4-oz. can diced green chiles
1 onion, chopped
2 T. chili powder
1 t. ground cumin
2 c. beef broth
salt and pepper to taste
6 to 8 6-inch corn tortillas,
  warmed
Garnish: shredded Cheddar
  cheese, shredded lettuce,
  sliced black olives,
  chopped tomato

Place roast in a slow cooker. Top
with remaining ingredients except
tortillas and garnish. Cover and cook
on low setting for 8 to 10 hours. With
2 forks, shred roast in slow cooker;
stir well. Spoon into warmed
tortillas; add desired garnishes.
Makes 6 to 8 servings.

Lisa Sett
Thousand Oaks, CA
My family asks for this
often...it smells so
good while it's cooking!
Add a side of beans and
dinner is served.

127

Country-Style Bread Pudding

3/4 c. brown sugar, packed
8 slices cinnamon-raisin bread,
   buttered and cubed
4 eggs, beaten
3-1/2 c. milk
1-1/2 t. vanilla extract
Garnish: whipped topping

Sprinkle brown sugar in a slow cooker that has been sprayed with non-stick vegetable spray. Add bread to slow cooker. Whisk together remaining ingredients except whipped cream; pour over bread. Cover and cook on high setting for 2 to 3 hours, until thickened. Do not stir. Spoon pudding into individual bowls. Drizzle brown sugar sauce from slow cooker over pudding. Garnish with dollops of whipped topping. Makes 8 to 10 servings.

Patricia Wissler
Harrisburg, PA

This is the best-tasting bread pudding ever, and so much easier than making it in the oven.

Beans & Weenies

1 lb. hot dogs, sliced
3 16-oz. cans pork & beans
1/4 c. onion, chopped
1/2 c. catsup
1/4 c. molasses
2 t. mustard

Combine all ingredients in a slow cooker; stir well. Cover and cook on low setting for 3 to 4 hours. Makes 6 to 8 servings.

Sharon Crider
Junction City, KS

A year 'round favorite...
a standby for summer
picnics, yet hearty and
satisfying during cold
weather too!

BBQ Pulled-Pork Fajitas

2-1/2 lb. boneless pork loin
   roast, trimmed
1 onion, thinly sliced
2 c. barbecue sauce
3/4 c. chunky salsa
1 T. chili powder
1 t. ground cumin
16-oz. pkg. frozen stir-fry
   peppers and onions
1/2 t. salt
18 8 to 10-inch flour tortillas,
   warmed

Place roast in a slow cooker; top with onion. Mix sauce, salsa and spices; pour over roast. Cover and cook on low setting for 8 to 10 hours. Remove roast and place on a cutting board; shred, using 2 forks. Return to slow cooker and mix well; add stir-fry vegetables and salt. Increase setting to high; cover and cook for an additional 30 minutes, until hot and vegetables are tender. With a slotted spoon, fill each warmed tortilla with 1/2 cup pork mixture. Makes 18 servings.

Jackie Valvardi
Haddon Heights, NJ

We like to spice these up with shredded Pepper Jack cheese, guacamole and sour cream.

Texas Queso Dip

1 lb. hot ground pork sausage,
   browned and drained
32-oz. pkg. pasteurized process
   cheese spread, cubed
10-oz. can diced tomatoes
   with green chiles
1/2 c. milk
white corn tortilla chips

Combine all ingredients except
tortilla chips in a slow cooker.
Cover and cook on low setting
until cheese is melted, about
2 hours. Serve with tortilla chips.
Makes 10 to 12 servings.

131

Amy Shilliday
San Antonio, TX

Everyone will love
this dip...once they
sample it, be ready
to share the recipe!

Family Favorite Party Mix ▶

1 c. bite-size crispy wheat
    cereal squares
1 c. bite-size crispy rice
    cereal squares
1 c. bite-size crispy corn
    cereal squares
1 c. peanuts
1 c. pretzel sticks
1/4 c. butter, melted
2 T. Worcestershire sauce
1 t. seasoned salt
1 t. garlic salt
1 c. candy-coated chocolates
1 c. raisins

Combine cereals, nuts and pretzels in a slow cooker. Mix together butter, sauce and salts; gently stir into cereal mixture. Cover and cook on low setting for 3 to 4 hours. Uncover and cook on low setting for an additional 30 minutes; stir occasionally. Drain on paper towel-lined baking sheets; transfer to a large bowl. Cool. Add chocolates and raisins; toss to mix. Store in an airtight container.
Makes 7 cups.

Nola Coons
Gooseberry Patch
A no-watch, fix & forget version of this crunchy party starter!

Pizza Fondue

28-oz. jar spaghetti sauce
16-oz. pkg. shredded mozzarella
  cheese
1/4 c. grated Parmesan cheese
2 T. dried oregano
2 T. dried parsley
1 T. garlic powder
1 t. dried, minced onion
Italian bread cubes, pepperoni
  chunks, whole mushrooms,
  green pepper slices

Combine sauce, cheeses and
seasonings in a slow cooker; mix
well. Cover and cook on low setting
for 2 hours, until warmed through
and cheese is melted; stir. Serve with
desired dippers. Makes 10 servings.

133

Shannon Finewood
Corpus Christi, TX
Try dipping warm bread
sticks or crisp pretzel
rods into this fondue.

Peanutty Clusters

2 lbs. white melting chocolate,
   chopped
4 1-oz. sqs. bittersweet baking
   chocolate, chopped
12-oz. pkg. semi-sweet
   chocolate chips
24-oz. jar dry-roasted peanuts

Combine all ingredients except nuts
in a slow cooker. Cover and cook on
high setting for one hour. Reduce
setting to low; cover and cook an
additional hour, or until chocolates
are melted, stirring every 15 minutes.
Stir in nuts. Drop by teaspoonfuls
onto wax paper; let stand until set.
Store covered at room temperature.
Makes 3 to 4 dozen pieces.

Margaret Erhardt
Beavercreek, OH

For a special candy-box
finish, drop by spoonfuls
into mini paper muffin
cup liners.

Toffee Fondue

14-oz. pkg. caramels, unwrapped
1/4 c. milk
1/4 c. strong black coffee
1/2 c. milk chocolate chips
apple wedges, banana chunks,
    marshmallows, angel food
    cake cubes

Mix together caramels, milk, coffee
and chocolate chips in a small slow
cooker. Cover and cook on low
setting until melted, 2 to 3 hours.
Stir well. Serve with fruit,
marshmallows and cake cubes for
dipping. Makes about 10 servings.

135

Michelle Riihl
Windom, MN
Just perfect for sharing
with girlfriends! Try
dipping pretzel twists
too...the salty-sweet
combo is delectable.

Just Peachy Cider

4 5-1/2 oz. cans peach nectar
2 c. apple cider
3/4 t. pumpkin pie spice
4 slices orange

In a slow cooker, combine nectar,
juice and spice; top with orange slices.
Cover and cook on low setting for
4 to 6 hours. Stir before serving.
Serves 4.

Jennie Gist
Gooseberry Patch

We ran across this little
farm stand with all
varieties of cider...
bing cherry, peach and
cinnamon apple. Yum!

Lemon-Poppy Seed Cake

Rogene Rogers
Bemidji, MN

An upside-down cake that makes its own custard-like topping...yum!

15.8-oz. lemon-poppy seed
   bread mix
1 egg, beaten
8-oz. container sour cream
1-1/4 c. water, divided
1 T. butter
1/2 c. sugar
1/4 c. lemon juice

Combine bread mix, egg, sour cream and 1/2 cup water in a mixing bowl. Stir until well moistened; spread in a lightly greased slow cooker. Combine remaining water and other ingredients in a small saucepan; bring to a boil. Pour boiling mixture over batter in slow cooker. Cover and cook on high setting for 2 to 2-1/2 hours, until edges are golden. Turn off slow cooker; let cake cool in slow cooker for about 30 minutes with lid ajar. When cool enough to handle, hold a large plate over top of slow cooker and invert to turn out cake. Serves 10 to 12.

Sunday Beef & Noodles

Peggy Donnally
Toledo, OH

Noodles and potatoes with beef gravy...that's my idea of heaven on a plate!

2-lb. beef chuck roast
4 c. beef broth
1 c. onion, chopped
2 t. onion powder
1 t. garlic powder
1 T. dried parsley
salt and pepper to taste
16-oz. pkg. extra-wide
   egg noodles, cooked
mashed potatoes

Place roast in a slow cooker. Combine broth, onion and seasonings; pour over roast. Cover and cook on low setting for 6 to 8 hours. Remove roast; slice and return to slow cooker. Add noodles to slow cooker; heat through. Serve over mashed potatoes. Serves 6.

Glazed Carrots:

16-oz. pkg. baby carrots
1/2 c. orange juice
5 T. brown sugar, packed
2 T. butter
1/8 t. salt

Cover carrots with water in a saucepan. Cook until tender; drain. Add juice to saucepan; simmer until almost evaporated. Stir in remaining ingredients; cook until well blended and glazed. Serves 6.

Provincial Chicken

4 boneless, skinless chicken
  breasts
2 15-oz. cans diced tomatoes
2 zucchini, diced
10-3/4 oz. can cream of
  chicken soup
2 T. balsamic vinegar
1 T. dried, minced onion
2 T. dried parsley
1 t. dried basil
1 c. shredded Cheddar cheese
1/2 c. sour cream
cooked bowtie pasta

139

In a slow cooker, combine chicken, tomatoes, zucchini, soup, vinegar, onion and herbs. Cover and cook on low setting for 6 to 8 hours. Remove chicken, cut into bite-size pieces and return to slow cooker. Stir in cheese and sour cream; cover and cook for an additional 15 minutes. To serve, spoon over cooked pasta. Serves 6.

Shari Upchurch
Dearing, GA

I've tweaked this recipe over the years...now it's just the way my family likes it!

Slow-Cooker Mac & Cheese

8-oz. pkg. elbow macaroni, cooked
2 T. oil
12-oz. can evaporated milk
1-1/2 c. milk
3 c. pasteurized process cheese
   spread, shredded
1/4 c. butter, melted
2 T. dried, minced onion

Combine cooked macaroni and oil;
toss to coat. Pour into a lightly greased
slow cooker; stir in remaining
ingredients. Cover and cook on low
setting for 3 to 4 hours, stirring
occasionally. Serves 4 to 6.

Paula Schwenk
Pennsdale, PA

So cheesy and satisfying...
and it's a snap to
put together.

Colorado Pork Chops

6 bone-in pork chops,
   1-1/2 inches thick
15-oz. can chili beans with
   chili sauce
1-1/2 c. salsa
1 c. corn
Optional: green chiles to taste
cooked rice
Garnish: fresh cilantro

In a slow cooker, layer pork chops, beans, salsa, corn and chiles, if using. Cover and cook on low setting for 5 hours, or on high setting for 2-1/2 hours. Serve over cooked rice; garnish with cilantro. Serves 6.

141

Linda Wolfe
Westminster, CO
These tasty pork chops feature all the flavors of your favorite Mexican restaurant.

Brown Sugar Applesauce

3 lbs. cooking apples, cored,
  peeled and sliced
1/2 c. brown sugar, packed
1 t. cinnamon
1-1/2 T. lemon juice
Garnish: cinnamon

Combine all ingredients in a slow
cooker. Cover and cook on high setting
for 3 hours. Stir occasionally; mash
with a potato masher to desired
consistency. Sprinkle portions with
cinnamon. Makes 6 to 8 servings.

Gloria Smith
Webster, MA

Especially delicious with
roast pork! I like to use
Granny Smith apples for
this recipe.

Pot Roast & Dumplings

2 c. baby carrots
5 potatoes, peeled and halved
4-lb. beef chuck roast
garlic salt and pepper to taste
2 c. water
1-oz. pkg. onion soup mix

Place carrots and potatoes in a slow cooker. Place roast on top; sprinkle with garlic salt and pepper. Stir together water and soup mix; pour over roast. Cover and cook on low setting for 6 to 8 hours. Drain most of broth from slow cooker into a large soup pot; bring to a boil over medium-high heat. Drop dumpling batter into boiling broth by teaspoonfuls. Cover and cook for 15 minutes. Serve dumplings with roast and vegetables. Serves 8 to 10.

Dumplings:

2 c. all-purpose flour
1/2 t. salt
3 T. baking powder
1 c. light cream

Sift together dry ingredients. Add cream and stir quickly to make a medium-soft batter.

143

Wendy Sensing
Brentwood, TN

This is one of our favorite meals on a chilly day...at the end of a busy day, dinner is practically ready!

Garlic Smashed Potatoes

3 lbs. redskin potatoes, quartered
4 cloves garlic, minced
2 T. olive oil
1 t. salt
1/2 c. water
1/2 c. spreadable cream cheese with
   chives and onions
1/4 to 1/2 c. milk

Place potatoes in a slow cooker. Add garlic, oil, salt and water; mix well to coat potatoes. Cover and cook on high setting for 3-1/2 to 4-1/2 hours, until potatoes are tender. Mash potatoes with a potato masher or fork. Stir in cream cheese until well blended; add enough milk for a soft consistency. Serve immediately, or keep warm for up to 2 hours in slow cooker on low setting. Makes 4 to 6 servings.

Nancy Girard
Chesapeake, VA

This convenient recipe
has become one of
our favorites!

Rosemary & Thyme Chicken

3-lb. roasting chicken
1 to 2 T. garlic, minced
kosher salt to taste
1/2 onion, sliced into wedges
4 sprigs fresh rosemary
3 sprigs fresh thyme
seasoning salt to taste

Rub inside of chicken with garlic and kosher salt. Stuff with onion wedges and herb sprigs. Sprinkle seasoning salt on the outside of chicken; place in a slow cooker. Cover and cook on low setting for 8 to 10 hours. Serves 4.

145

Linda Sather
Moscow, OR

My family loves this chicken, made with fresh herbs from my garden.

Southern Chicken & Dumplings

3 10-3/4 oz. cans cream of
   chicken soup
1/4 c. onion, diced
6 boneless, skinless chicken breasts
3-3/4 c. water
3 12-oz. tubes refrigerated
   biscuits, quartered

Pour soup into a slow cooker; add onion and chicken. Pour in enough water to cover chicken. Cover and cook on low setting for 6 to 8 hours, or on high setting for 4 to 6 hours. About 45 minutes before serving, turn slow cooker to high setting. Remove chicken with a slotted spoon; shred into bite-size pieces and return to slow cooker. Drop biscuit quarters into slow cooker; stir well. Replace lid and cook for 35 minutes more, or until dumplings are done. Stir and serve. Serves 6 to 8.

Stephanie Lucius
Powder Springs, GA

A scrumptious-tasting
homemade dish...with
almost no effort!

Bayou Chicken

3 boneless, skinless chicken
    breasts, cubed
14-1/2 oz. can chicken broth
14-1/2 oz. can diced tomatoes
10-3/4 oz. can tomato soup
1/2 lb. smoked pork sausage,
    sliced
1/2 c. cooked ham, diced
1 onion, chopped
2 t. Cajun seasoning
hot pepper sauce to taste
cooked rice

Combine all ingredients except rice
in a slow cooker; stir. Cover and
cook on low setting for 8 hours.
Serve over cooked rice. Serves 6 to 8.

147

Dawn Dhooghe
Concord, NC

The slow cooker always seems
to be going at our house.
This is one of my husband's
favorites...and it's so
easy to put together!

German Roast Pork & Sauerkraut

3 to 4-lb. boneless pork roast
salt and pepper to taste
1 T. shortening
32-oz. pkg. sauerkraut
2 apples, cored, peeled and
    quartered
1 c. apple juice or water
14-oz. pkg. frozen pierogies

Sprinkle roast with salt and pepper.
Heat shortening in a skillet over
medium-high heat. Brown roast on
all sides; place in a slow cooker. Add
undrained sauerkraut, apples and juice
or water; blend. Gently add pierogies
so they are partly submerged in the
sauerkraut (as the roast cooks, more
liquid will cover the pierogies). Cover
and cook on low setting for 8 to
9 hours. Serves 4 to 6.

Sherry Doherty
Medford, NJ
A delicious one-pot dinner
for New Year's Day
or any time of year.

Praline Apple Crisp ▶

6 Granny Smith or Braeburn
  apples, cored, peeled and
  sliced
1 t. cinnamon
1/2 c. quick-cooking oats,
  uncooked
1/3 c. brown sugar, packed
1/4 c. all-purpose flour
1/2 c. chilled butter, diced
1/2 c. chopped pecans
1/2 c. toffee baking bits
Optional: whipped topping

Toss together apples and cinnamon.
Place in a slow cooker that has been
sprayed with non-stick vegetable
spray; set aside. Combine oats,
brown sugar, flour and butter; mix
with a pastry cutter or fork until
crumbly. Stir in pecans and toffee
bits; sprinkle over apples. Cover and
cook on low setting for 4 to 6 hours.
Top with whipped topping, if
desired. Makes 10 servings.

Katie Majeske
Denver, PA

What's more comforting than
warm apple crisp? I often
make this for work, church,
potlucks or family.

Magic Meatloaf

2 lbs. ground beef
1 egg, beaten
1/2 c. green pepper, chopped
1/2 c. onion, chopped
1 c. milk
1 c. saltine cracker crumbs
.87-oz. pkg. brown gravy mix
1-1/2 t. salt
6 to 8 new redskin potatoes

Mix all ingredients except potatoes in a large bowl. Mix well and form into a loaf; place in a lightly greased slow cooker. Arrange potatoes around meatloaf. Cover and cook on low setting for 8 to 10 hours, or on high setting for 3 to 5 hours. Serves 4 to 6.

Beverly Tierney
Greenfield, IN

This is such a comforting dish and so nice to come home to. The meatloaf is so very flavorful and juicy... really wonderful!

Chicken Cacciatore

Mary Whitacre
Mount Vernon, OH

Every time I make this, my family just swoons! It is delicious any time of the year and is so easy.

1 lb. boneless, skinless chicken breasts
26-oz. jar chunky garden vegetable spaghetti sauce
1 zucchini, chopped
1 green pepper, chopped
1 sweet onion, chopped
cooked rotini pasta
Garnish: chopped black olives, shredded Parmesan cheese

Place chicken in a slow cooker; pour sauce over top. Add vegetables. Cover and cook on low setting for 6 to 8 hours. To serve, spoon over cooked pasta. Garnish with olives and Parmesan cheese. Serves 4.

151

Savory Rice Pilaf

3/4 c. long-cooking wild rice,
  uncooked
1/2 c. long-cooking brown rice,
  uncooked
1/2 lb. portabella mushrooms,
  sliced 1-inch thick
10-3/4 oz. can cream of
  mushroom soup with
  roasted garlic
1-1/2 c. water
1/8 t. pepper

Combine all ingredients in a slow cooker; stir well. Cover and cook on low setting for 6 to 7 hours, until rice is tender. Serves 6 to 8.

Cathy Hillier
Salt Lake City, UT

The blend of mushrooms, wild and brown rice make this a great side dish for beef, poultry, seafood or pork.

Best-Ever Lasagna

1 lb. ground beef, browned
   and drained
1 t. Italian seasoning
8 lasagna noodles, uncooked
   and broken into thirds
28-oz. jar spaghetti sauce
1/3 c. water
4-oz. can sliced mushrooms,
   drained
15-oz. container ricotta cheese
8-oz. pkg. shredded mozzarella
   cheese
Garnish: shredded Parmesan
   cheese

Combine ground beef and Italian seasoning. Arrange half of the lasagna noodles in a greased slow cooker. Spread half of the ground beef mixture over noodles. Top with half each of remaining ingredients except Parmesan cheese. Repeat layering process. Cover and cook on low setting for 5 hours. Garnish with Parmesan cheese. Serves 10.

153

Cherylann Smith
Efland, NC

This is a quick, easy recipe for homestyle lasagna...just add garlic bread and a tossed salad.

Pumpkin Pie Pudding

15-oz. can pumpkin
12-oz. can evaporated milk
3/4 c. sugar
1/2 c. biscuit baking mix
2 eggs, beaten
2 T. butter, melted
2-1/2 t. pumpkin pie spice
2 t. vanilla extract
Garnish: whipped cream

In a bowl, mix together all ingredients except topping. Transfer to a slow cooker that has been sprayed with non-stick vegetable spray. Cover and cook on low setting for 3-1/2 to 4 hours. Pudding will start to pull away from sides of slow cooker; test for doneness with a toothpick inserted in center. Serve warm, topped with dollops of whipped cream. Makes 4 to 6 servings.

Lana Rulevish
Ashley, IL
I received this recipe from a friend I met online. It is very good!

Cran-Orange Turkey Breast

3 to 4-lb. boneless turkey breast
1/2 c. orange juice
1.35-oz. pkg. onion soup mix
15-oz. can whole-berry cranberry
   sauce

Place turkey breast in a slow cooker.
Combine remaining ingredients;
pour over turkey. Cover and cook on
high setting for one hour; reduce to
low setting and cook for an additional
6 hours. Serves 6.

155

Jeanie Petersen
Saint Charles, IL

My son requested a slow
cooker primarily for this
recipe! He has also shared
the recipe as well as the
meal with friends.

Corned Beef Dinner

4 c. hot water
2 T. cider vinegar
1 c. carrots, peeled and sliced
1 onion, cut in wedges
1/2 t. pepper
3-lb. corned beef with spice packet
8 redskin potatoes, quartered
1 head cabbage, cut into wedges

In a slow cooker, combine water, vinegar, carrots, onion and pepper. Top with corned beef, contents of spice packet, potatoes and cabbage. Cover and cook on low setting for 8 to 10 hours. Serves 6 to 8.

Karen Alexander
Navarre, OH

Delicious any time of the year...so easy to prepare in a slow cooker!

Ham & Ranch Potatoes

2 lbs. redskin potatoes, peeled and quartered
8-oz. pkg. cream cheese, softened
1-oz. pkg. buttermilk ranch salad dressing mix
10-3/4 oz. can cream of potato soup
16-oz. pkg. cooked ham, cubed
1 c. shredded Cheddar cheese
salt and pepper to taste

Place potatoes in a slow cooker. Combine cream cheese and dressing mix; add soup and mix well. Add cream cheese mixture to slow cooker and mix with potatoes. Cover and cook on low setting for 6-1/2 hours. Stir in ham and top with cheese; add salt and pepper to taste. Cover and cook for another 15 to 30 minutes, until cheese is melted. Serves 6.

157

Hope Davenport
Portland, TX

My family loves this dish and it's so easy to make. The dressing mix gives it a wonderful flavor.

Country Captain

2 T. olive oil
3-lb. chicken, quartered and
   skin removed
2 cloves garlic, minced
1 onion, chopped
1 green pepper, chopped
1/2 c. celery, chopped
2 t. curry powder
1/3 c. currants or raisins
14-1/2 oz. can whole tomatoes,
   chopped
1 t. sugar
salt and pepper to taste
cooked rice
Garnish: 1/4 c. slivered almonds

Heat oil in a skillet over medium heat.
Sauté chicken just until golden; place
in a slow cooker and set aside. Add
garlic, onion, green pepper, celery and
curry powder to skillet; sauté briefly.
Remove from heat; stir in remaining
ingredients except rice and almonds.
Pour over chicken. Cover and cook on
low setting for 6 hours. Serve over
cooked rice; sprinkle with almonds.
Makes 4 servings.

Marlene Darnell
Newport Beach, CA
We discovered this curry-
flavored dish with the
unusual name on a trip to
southern Georgia.

Pepper Steak

1 to 1-1/2 lbs. beef round steak,
　cut into bite-size pieces
1/3 c. all-purpose flour
1/4 t. pepper
1 onion, sliced
1 green and/or red pepper, sliced
14-1/2 oz. can diced tomatoes
4-oz. can sliced mushrooms,
　drained
3 T. soy sauce
cooked rice

Place roast in a slow cooker.
Sprinkle with flour and pepper;
stir well to coat meat. Add remaining
ingredients except rice. Cover and
cook on high setting for one hour;
reduce to low setting and cook for
an additional 8 hours. Serve over
cooked rice. Makes 4 to 6 servings.

159

Zoe Groff
Saybrook, IL

This hearty dish is sure to
be a hit at any party...and
they'll never know it only
took you 10 minutes to put
it together!

Garlicky Herbed Pork Roast

4 to 5-lb. pork roast
4 cloves garlic, slivered
1 t. dried thyme
1/2 t. dried sage
1/2 t. ground cloves
1 t. salt
1 t. lemon zest
2 T. cold water
2 T. cornstarch

Cut 16 small pockets into roast with a knife tip; insert garlic slivers. Combine seasonings and zest; rub over roast. Place roast in a slow cooker. Cover and cook on low setting for 7 to 9 hours, or on high setting for 4 to 5 hours. Allow roast to stand 10 to 15 minutes before slicing. Remove and discard garlic pieces. Strain juices into a saucepan over medium heat; bring to a boil. Mix together water and cornstarch until dissolved; gradually add to saucepan. Cook until thickened, about 5 minutes. Serve gravy over sliced pork. Serves 8 to 10.

Nancy Wise
Little Rock, AR
This recipe is one I know I can count on when I want a dinner that's really special.

Down-Home Chicken & Noodles

1 lb. boneless, skinless chicken
   breasts
salt and pepper to taste
2 10-3/4 oz. cans cream of
   chicken soup
14-1/2 oz. can chicken broth
16-oz. pkg. wide egg noodles,
   cooked

Place chicken in a slow cooker;
sprinkle with salt and pepper. Top
with soup. Cover and cook on low
setting for 6 hours, or until chicken
is very tender. Remove chicken from
slow cooker and shred; return to
slow cooker. Add broth and cooked
noodles; mix well. Cover and cook
on low setting for an additional
30 minutes, or until heated through.
Serves 6.

161

Alicia Palmer
Greenville, OH

My family just loves this
dish...it tastes like
you've been cooking
all day!

Mom's Blueberry Cobbler

2 8-oz. tubes refrigerated biscuits,
  quartered and divided
1/3 c. brown sugar, packed
1/2 t. cinnamon
1/3 c. butter, melted
21-oz. can blueberry pie filling,
  divided

Layer one tube of biscuits in a slow
cooker that has been sprayed with
non-stick vegetable spray. In a small
bowl, mix together brown sugar,
cinnamon and butter just until
combined; sprinkle half of mixture
over biscuits. Spread half of pie filling
over top. Layer with remaining
biscuits; sprinkle with remaining
brown sugar mixture and top with
remaining pie filling. Cover and cook
on high setting for 2-1/2 to 3 hours,
until biscuits are golden. Makes 6 to
8 servings.

Sharon Tillman
Hampton, VA

Growing up, I always loved
blueberries...I still do!
Mom would make this easy
recipe for me year 'round.

Honey-Mustard Short Ribs

3 to 4 lbs. bone-in beef
   short ribs
salt and pepper to taste
1 c. hickory smoke-flavored
   barbecue sauce
3 T. honey
1 T. Dijon mustard
3 cloves garlic, minced
2 T. cornstarch
2 T. cold water

Sprinkle ribs with salt and pepper;
place in a slow cooker and set aside.
Combine barbecue sauce, honey,
mustard, garlic and additional salt
and pepper, if desired; pour over
ribs. Cover and cook on low setting
for 6 to 7 hours. During the last
30 minutes of cooking, whisk
cornstarch into water. Add to slow
cooker, stirring until thickened.
Serves 4.

163

David Wink
Marion, OH

All the fun of a
Saturday night barbecue...
none of the effort!

White Bean & Sausage Stew

6 Italian pork sausage links
1/4 c. water
1 T. olive oil
1 onion, chopped
1 clove garlic, chopped
2 15-oz. cans Great Northern
   beans, drained and rinsed
28-oz. can chopped tomatoes,
   drained
1 t. dried thyme
salt and pepper to taste

Pierce sausages and place in a large skillet. Add water; bring to a boil over medium heat. Reduce heat and simmer for 10 minutes, turning occasionally. Transfer sausages to a plate. Heat oil in skillet over medium-high heat; sauté onion and garlic. Stir in beans, tomatoes and thyme. Add half of bean mixture to a slow cooker; arrange sausages on top. Spread remaining bean mixture over sausages. Cover and cook on high setting. Check after 2 hours; stir in additional water, if needed. Remove sausages; slice into thick chunks and return to slow cooker. Sprinkle with salt and pepper. Serves 4.

Diane Cohen
The Woodlands, TX

Add a basket of warm, buttered biscuits for a satisfying soup supper.

Country Chicken Stew

4 boneless, skinless chicken
   thighs
3-1/2 c. chicken broth
2 c. plum tomatoes, chopped
1 c. green pepper, chopped
1 c. onion, chopped
1/2 c. long-cooking rice,
   uncooked
1/2 c. canned garbanzo beans,
   drained and rinsed
3 cloves garlic, chopped
1/2 t. salt
1/2 t. pepper
1 bay leaf
Garnish: shredded Monterey
   Jack cheese, diced avocado

Combine all ingredients except
garnish in a slow cooker. Cover and
cook on low setting for 7 to 9 hours,
until chicken and rice are tender.
Discard bay leaf. To serve, place a
chicken thigh in each soup bowl; top
with soup and garnish as desired.
Serves 4.

Kay Marone
Des Moines, IA
A savory, filling meal
in a bowl.

165

Creamy Potato Soup

6 potatoes, peeled and cubed
2 onions, chopped
1 carrot, sliced
1 stalk celery, sliced
4 cubes chicken bouillon
1 T. dried parsley
5 c. water
1/4 t. pepper
1 T. salt
1/3 c. butter, melted
12-oz. can evaporated milk

Combine all ingredients except evaporated milk in a slow cooker. Cover and cook on low setting for 10 to 12 hours, or on high setting for 3 to 4 hours. Stir in milk during last hour of cooking. Serves 6.

Roberta Simpkins
Mentor-on-the-Lake, OH

Garnish with a sprinkle of snipped fresh chives.

Tami's Taco Soup

1 lb. ground turkey, browned
   and drained
32-oz. carton chicken broth
2 14-1/2 oz. cans petite diced
   tomatoes with green chiles
15.8-oz. can Great Northern
   beans, drained and rinsed
15-oz. can black beans, drained
   and rinsed
15-1/4 oz. can yellow hominy,
   drained
15-1/4 oz. can white hominy,
   drained
1-1/4 oz. pkg. taco seasoning mix
1-oz. pkg. ranch salad dressing
   mix
Garnish: shredded Cheddar
   cheese

Combine all ingredients except
cheese in a slow cooker. Cover and
cook on low setting for 4 to 5 hours.
To serve, top with cheese and Tortilla
Strips. Serves 8 to 10.

Tortilla Strips:

3 corn tortillas, sliced into strips
oil for frying

Fry strips in oil until crisp; drain.

167

Tami Bowman
Marysville, OH
I make this soup often...
my "boys" are very picky
and all 3 of us like this,
which is rare!

Old-Fashioned Bean Soup

16-oz. pkg. dried navy beans
2 qts. water
1 meaty ham bone
1 onion, chopped
1/2 c. celery leaves, chopped
5 whole peppercorns
salt to taste
Optional: bay leaf

Cover beans with water in a large soup pot; soak overnight. Drain. Combine beans, 2 quarts water and remaining ingredients in a slow cooker. Cover and cook on low setting for 10 to 12 hours, or on high setting for 5 to 6 hours. Remove ham bone; dice meat and return to slow cooker. Discard bay leaf, if using. Makes 8 to 10 servings.

Easy Cornbread:

8-1/2 oz. pkg. corn muffin mix
8-1/2 oz. pkg. yellow cake mix
2 eggs, beaten
1/3 c. milk
1/2 c. water

Combine all ingredients; mix well. Spread batter in a greased 13"x9" baking pan. Bake at 350 degrees for 15 to 20 minutes. Makes 10 to 12 servings.

Kathleen Poritz
Burlington, WI

I'm a teacher's aide with winter recess duty... a cup of bean soup warms the body & soul!

Game-Day Corn Chowder

1 lb. smoked pork sausage
3 c. frozen hashbrowns with
    onions and peppers
2 carrots, peeled and chopped
15-oz. can creamed corn
10-3/4 oz. can cream of
    mushroom soup with
    roasted garlic
2 c. water

Brown sausage in a skillet over medium heat; drain and cut into bite-size pieces. Place sausage in a slow cooker; top with hashbrowns and carrots. Combine corn, soup and water; stir until blended and pour over sausage mixture. Cover and cook on low setting for 8 to 10 hours. Serves 6.

169

Jo Ann

This savory chowder is always simmering away in my slow cooker on football Saturday mornings so it's ready to enjoy by kick-off.

Green Chile Stew

1 to 1-1/2 lbs. boneless pork,
  cubed
2 16-oz. cans pinto beans
2 14-1/2 oz. cans Mexican-style
  diced tomatoes
2 4-oz. cans diced green chiles
15-1/2 oz. can hominy, drained
1 t. ground cumin
salt and pepper to taste

Place pork in a slow cooker. Top with
remaining ingredients; stir. Cover and
cook on high setting for 4 to 5 hours.
Serves 4.

Linda Neel
Lovington, NM

Perfect for a cold evening!
Use hot, medium or mild
green chiles according to
your own taste.

French Onion Soup

1/4 c. butter
3 c. onion, sliced
1 T. sugar
1 t. salt
2 T. all-purpose flour
4 c. beef broth
1/4 c. dry white wine or
   beef broth
6 slices French bread
1/2 c. grated Parmesan cheese
1/2 c. shredded mozzarella cheese

171

Melt butter in a skillet over medium heat. Add onion; cook for 15 to 20 minutes, until soft. Stir in sugar and salt; continue to cook and stir until golden. Add flour; mix well. Combine onion mixture, broth and wine or broth in a slow cooker. Cover and cook on high setting for 3 to 4 hours. Ladle soup into oven-proof bowls. Top with bread slices; sprinkle with cheeses. Broil until cheese is bubbly and melted. Serves 6.

Robin Hill
Rochester, NY

Now you can enjoy this elegant soup any time and it's so easy to prepare.

Southern BBQ Bean Soup

16-oz pkg. Great Northern beans
3/4 c. onion, chopped
1/8 t. pepper
2 lbs. beef short ribs, cut into
    serving-size pieces
6 c. water
1 c. barbecue sauce
1 to 2 t. salt

Cover beans with water in a large soup pot; soak overnight. Drain. Combine beans, onion, pepper and short ribs in a slow cooker; add enough water to cover. Cover and cook on low setting for 10 to 12 hours. Remove short ribs; cut meat from bones. Return meat to slow cooker; stir in sauce and salt to taste. Cover and cook on high setting for an additional 20 minutes, until warmed through. Serves 6 to 8.

Tori Willis
Champaign, IL

When my daughter visited Alabama, this was one recipe she brought home... it's becoming a family favorite up north too!

Chuck Wagon Stew

1-1/2 lbs. stew beef, cubed
1/2 lb. smoked pork sausage,
  sliced
1 onion, chopped
3 potatoes, peeled and cubed
28-oz. can barbecue baked beans

Place beef, sausage, onion and
potatoes into a slow cooker; mix
well. Spoon beans over top. Cover
and cook on low setting for 8 to
10 hours, or on high setting 4 to
5 hours. Stir again before serving.
Makes 6 servings.

173

**Peggy Pelfrey
Fort Riley, KS**
This hearty stew is ideal
for a fall social or a
weekend at the cabin.

Black Bean Chili

1-lb. pork tenderloin
3 15-1/2 oz. cans black beans,
   drained and rinsed
16-oz. jar chunky salsa
1/2 c. chicken broth
1 green pepper, chopped
1 onion, chopped
2 t. chili powder
1 t. ground cumin
1 t. dried oregano
Garnish: sour cream, diced
   tomatoes

Place pork in a lightly greased slow
cooker; add remaining ingredients
except garnish. Cover and cook
on low setting for 8 hours, or on high
setting for 4 hours. Shred pork; return
to slow cooker. Garnish servings with
dollops of sour cream and diced
tomatoes. Serves 4 to 6.

Darrell Lawry
Kissimmee, FL

A different kind of chili!
I like to top the bowl
with a handful of
crushed tortilla chips.

Down-on-the-Bayou Gumbo

3 T. all-purpose flour
3 T. oil
3 c. chicken broth
1/2 lb. smoked pork sausage,
   sliced
2 c. frozen okra
14-1/2 oz. can diced tomatoes
1 onion, chopped
1 green pepper, chopped
3 cloves garlic, minced
1/4 t. cayenne pepper
3/4 lb. cooked medium
   shrimp, tails removed
cooked rice

175

Stir together flour and oil in a
saucepan over medium heat. Cook,
stirring constantly, for 5 minutes.
Reduce heat; cook and stir for
10 minutes, until mixture is reddish
brown. Pour broth into a slow
cooker; stir in flour mixture. Add
remaining ingredients except shrimp
and rice. Cover and cook on low
setting for 7 to 9 hours. Shortly
before serving, add shrimp to slow
cooker; mix well. Cover and cook
on low setting for about 20 minutes.
Ladle gumbo over cooked rice in
soup bowls. Serves 6.

Sue Neely
Greenville, IL
You can't help but smile
with a bowl of gumbo in
front of you!

Grama's Minestrone Soup

1/4 c. zesty Italian salad dressing
1 c. onion, chopped
1/2 c. celery, chopped
1/2 c. carrot, peeled and chopped
14-1/2 oz. can diced tomatoes
15-1/2 oz. can kidney beans,
   drained and rinsed
2 14-oz. cans vegetable broth
3 c. water
1 t. Italian seasoning
12-oz. pkg. small shell pasta,
   uncooked and divided

Combine all ingredients except pasta
in a slow cooker; mix well. Cover and
cook on low setting for 8 hours. Measure
out 1-1/2 cups pasta, reserving the rest
for another recipe. Stir uncooked
pasta into slow cooker. Cover and
cook on high setting for an additional
30 minutes, or until pasta is tender.
Serves 6.

Lori Czarnecki
Milwaukee, WI

This is a recipe my
grandmother used to make on
the stovetop...I adapted it
to the slow cooker.

Turkey & Wild Rice Soup

1/2 c. onion, chopped
2 t. oil
1 c. deli smoked turkey, diced
1 c. celery, diced
1 c. carrots, peeled and diced
1/2 c. long-cooking wild rice,
   uncooked
1 t. dried tarragon
1/4 t. pepper
2 14-oz. cans chicken broth
12-oz. can evaporated milk
1/3 c. all-purpose flour
1 c. frozen peas, thawed
Optional: 2 T. dry sherry

177

In a skillet over medium heat, cook onion in oil for about 4 minutes, until tender. Combine onion with turkey, celery, carrots, rice and seasonings in a slow cooker; stir in broth. Cover and cook on low setting for 6 to 8 hours. Mix evaporated milk and flour; stir into soup along with peas and sherry, if using. Cover and cook on low setting for about 20 minutes, until thickened. Makes 6 servings.

Judith Jennings
Ironwood, MI

This hearty soup is chock-full of veggies! Make it even healthier with fat-free broth and evaporated milk, if you like.

Down-Home Pea Soup

8 c. water
2 c. dried split peas
1-1/2 c. celery, sliced
1-1/2 c. carrots, peeled
  and sliced
1 onion, sliced
2 bay leaves
salt and pepper to taste
1 to 2 c. cooked ham, cubed

Combine all ingredients in a slow cooker. Cover and cook on low for 4 to 6 hours. Discard bay leaves before serving. Makes 8 to 10 servings.

Jude Trimnal
Brevard, NC

Our parents made this soup often. It is delicious year 'round, but is especially warming on winter days.

Italian Chicken Stew

3 to 4 boneless, skinless chicken
   breasts
2 48-oz. cans stewed tomatoes
20-oz. pkg. frozen Italian
   vegetables
1 clove garlic, minced
16-oz. pkg. rigatoni pasta,
   uncooked
Garnish: shredded mozzarella
   cheese, grated Parmesan
   cheese

Place chicken, tomatoes, vegetables
and garlic in a slow cooker. Cover
and cook on low setting for 4 to
5 hours. About 35 minutes before
cooking is complete, top stew with
uncooked pasta; do not stir. Cover
and finish cooking. Pasta will thicken
the stew as it cooks. Garnish portions
with cheeses. Makes 4 to 5 servings.

179

Lisanne Miller
Canton, MS

This version is quicker
than Grandma Oli's recipe,
but it sure has the same
great taste!

White Chili

16-oz. pkg. dried Great Northern
    beans
2 lbs. boneless, skinless chicken
    breasts, cubed
14-1/2 oz. can chicken broth
1 c. water
1 onion, chopped
3 cloves garlic, minced
2 4-oz. cans chopped green chiles
2 t. ground cumin
1-1/2 t. cayenne pepper
1 t. dried oregano
1/2 t. salt
Garnish: shredded Monterey Jack
    cheese, chopped green onions

Cover beans with water in a large
soup pot and soak overnight; drain.
Combine beans with remaining
ingredients except garnish in a slow
cooker and stir. Cover and cook on low
setting for 10 to 12 hours, or on high
for 5 to 6 hours, stirring occasionally.
Garnish individual portions as desired.
Serves 6 to 8.

Wendy West Hickey
Pittsburgh, PA

Speed up this recipe by
substituting canned
beans...you'll need about
three, 15-ounce cans. No
soaking required!

Chicken Noodle Soup

4 carrots, peeled and sliced
4 stalks celery, sliced
1 onion, chopped
2 bay leaves
1/2 t. dried thyme
4 t. salt
1/2 t. pepper
3-1/2 lb. chicken
7 to 8 c. chicken broth or water
12-oz. pkg. medium egg noodles,
    uncooked and divided

181

Place vegetables, seasonings and chicken in a slow cooker. Add enough broth or water to fill slow cooker 2/3 full. Cover and cook on low setting for 8 to 10 hours. Remove chicken and cool, reserving broth in slow cooker. Discard bones, skin and bay leaves. Measure out 3 cups noodles, reserving the rest for another recipe. Stir uncooked noodles into slow cooker. Cover and cook on low setting for 10 to 20 minutes, until tender. Shred chicken and stir back into soup. Makes 8 servings.

Dale-Harriet Rogovich
Madison, WI
At the first sign of sniffles, I put this soup on to simmer. It makes me feel much better in no time!

Chicken & Broccoli Chowder

1 lb. boneless, skinless chicken
   thighs, cubed
14-1/2 oz. can chicken broth
1/2 c. water
1 c. baby carrots, sliced
1 c. sliced mushrooms
1/2 c. onion, chopped
1/4 t. garlic powder
1/8 t. dried thyme
10-3/4 oz. can cream of chicken
   & broccoli soup
1/2 c. milk
3 T. all-purpose flour
10-oz. pkg. frozen chopped
   broccoli, thawed

Combine chicken, broth, water, carrots, mushrooms, onion and seasonings in a slow cooker; mix well. Cover and cook on low setting for 7 to 9 hours. In a bowl, whisk together soup, milk and flour; stir into slow cooker along with broccoli. Cover and cook an additional 30 minutes, or until broccoli is tender. Makes 4 to 6 servings.

Susie Backus
Gooseberry Patch

Warms you right down
to your toes!

Hearty Beef Stew

6 potatoes, peeled and cubed
6 carrots, peeled and cut into
   3-inch pieces
3 lbs. stew beef, cut into
   1-1/2 inch cubes
1/3 c. soy sauce
1 t. paprika
1 t. salt
1/2 t. pepper
3 T. all-purpose flour
12-oz. pkg. frozen chopped
   onions
10-1/2 oz. can beef broth
8-oz. can tomato sauce

183

Arrange potatoes in a slow cooker;
top with carrots. Add beef; sprinkle
with soy sauce, seasonings, flour and
onions. Combine broth and tomato
sauce; pour over top. Cover and cook
for 9 to 10 hours on low setting, or
4-1/2 to 5 hours on high setting.
Serves 8 to 10.

Maxie Martin
Granbury, TX
The night before, I do all
the peeling and chopping,
cover the potatoes with
water and place in the
fridge until morning.

Mom's Black-Eyed Pea Soup

16-oz. pkg. dried black-eyed peas
10-3/4 oz. can bean with bacon
  soup
4 c. water
6 carrots, peeled and chopped
2-lb. beef chuck roast, cubed
1/4 t. pepper

Combine dried peas and remaining
ingredients in a slow cooker; mix well.
Cover and cook on low setting for
9 to 10 hours. Makes 6 servings.

Dana Cunningham
Lafayette, LA

This is one recipe sure to
be found in every recipe
box in our family.

Rachel's Turkey Stew

28-oz. can turkey, drained and
   broth reserved
8-1/2 oz. can corn, drained and
   liquid reserved
1-1/2 c. frozen sliced carrots,
   thawed
14-1/2 oz. can chicken broth
1 c. buttermilk
1 T. dill weed
1/4 c. cornstarch

Mix together turkey, corn and
carrots in a slow cooker; set aside.
Whisk together reserved turkey
broth, chicken broth, reserved
corn liquid, buttermilk and dill
weed; pour over turkey mixture.
Cover and cook on low setting for
6 hours. Just before serving, stir in
cornstarch and cook until thickened.
Serves 6 to 8.

Rachel Boyd
Defiance, OH

I combined 2 recipes
to make this wonderful
stew. Now it's a family
favorite...even the
kids love it!

Everyone's Favorite Vegetable Soup

1 lb. stew beef, cubed
1 T. oil
4 potatoes, peeled and diced
16-oz. pkg. frozen peas
16-oz. pkg. frozen corn
16-oz. pkg. baby carrots
2 12-oz. jars beef gravy
2 15-oz. cans tomato sauce
salt and pepper to taste

In a skillet over medium heat, brown beef in oil; drain. Add potatoes to skillet; cook until softened. Combine beef mixture and remaining ingredients in a slow cooker. Cover and cook on low setting for 8 hours, or until tender, stirring occasionally. Makes 8 servings.

Marcel Beers
Easton, PA

Like a vegetable garden in a soup bowl...even my one-year-old likes it!

Savory Chicken Soup

2 carrots, peeled and sliced
2 stalks celery, chopped
2 to 3 potatoes, peeled and
   quartered
2 onions, sliced
3 boneless, skinless chicken
   breasts, cubed
14-1/2 oz. can chicken broth
2 c. water
1/4 t. salt
1/4 t. pepper
1/2 t. dried parsley
1/2 t. dried basil

187

Place vegetables in a slow cooker;
add chicken. Pour in broth and
water; sprinkle seasonings over top.
Cover and cook on low setting for
8 hours, or on high setting for
4 hours. Serves 4 to 6.

Estella Hickman
Galloway, OH

Oh, how the aroma of
this simmering soup
fills the kitchen.

Zesty Macaroni & Cheese

16-oz. pkg. elbow macaroni,
    cooked
16-oz. pkg. pasteurized processed
    cheese, cubed
8-oz. pkg. Pepper Jack cheese,
    cubed
2 10-3/4 oz. cans Cheddar
    cheese soup
1 c. onion, minced

Place macaroni and cheeses into a slow
cooker. Add soup and stir until coated
well; add onion. Cover and cook on
low setting for 5 to 6 hours, or on high
setting for 2 hours. Stir occasionally.
Makes 6 to 8 servings.

Jen Licon-Conner
Gooseberry Patch

Make this recipe extra
zesty...add 1/2 cup salsa
or stir in green chiles
to your taste!

Italian Scallion Meatballs

1 c. grape juice
1 c. apple jelly
1 c. catsup
8-oz. can tomato sauce
4 lbs. frozen Italian-style
    meatballs
Garnish: sliced green onions

In a small saucepan, combine all
ingredients except meatballs. Cook
and stir over medium heat until
jelly is melted; remove from heat.
Place meatballs in a slow cooker;
pour sauce over top and gently stir
to coat. Cover and cook on low
setting for 4 hours. Sprinkle with
onions at serving time. Makes
about 11 dozen.

189

Wendy Jacobs
Idaho Falls, ID

You can't go wrong
with this classic party
recipe...everyone
will love it.

Tex-Mex Chili Dogs

1-lb. pkg. hot dogs
2 15-oz. cans chili without beans
10-3/4 oz. can Cheddar cheese
   soup
4-oz. can chopped green chiles
10 hot dog buns, split
Garnish: chopped onion, crushed
   corn chips, shredded Cheddar
   cheese

Place hot dogs in a slow cooker. In
a separate bowl, combine chili, soup
and chiles; pour over hot dogs.
Cover and cook on low setting for
4 to 5 hours. Serve hot dogs in buns;
top with chili mixture and desired
garnishes. Makes 10 sandwiches.

Stacie Avner
Delaware, OH

Plain ol' chili dogs are
a thing of the past
at our house!

Anne's Chicken Burritos

6 boneless, skinless chicken
   breasts
15-1/4 oz. can corn, drained
16-oz. can black beans, drained
   and rinsed
16-oz. jar salsa
6 to 8 10-inch flour tortillas
Garnish: shredded Cheddar
   cheese, sour cream, salsa,
   guacamole

191

Place chicken in a slow cooker;
top with corn, beans and salsa.
Cover and cook on low setting for
8 to 10 hours, or on high setting for
4 to 6 hours. Shred chicken; stir back
into slow cooker. To serve, spoon
mixture onto tortillas. Add desired
garnishes and roll up. Serves 6 to 8.

Jennifer Sievers
Roselle, IL

My friend, Anne, gave me
this easy slow-cooker
recipe...we love it more
and more each time
we make it!

County Fair Italian Sausages

20-oz. pkg. Italian pork sausages
1 green pepper, sliced
1 onion, sliced
26-oz. jar spaghetti sauce
5 sub buns, split
Garnish: 5 slices Provolone cheese

Brown sausages in a non-stick skillet over medium heat; place in a slow cooker. Add pepper and onion; top with sauce. Cover and cook on low setting for 4 to 6 hours. To serve, place sausages in buns; top with sauce mixture and cheese. Makes 5 sandwiches.

Dale Duncan
Waterloo, IA

Our family always heads to the Italian sausage food tent at the fair... with this recipe, we can have them anytime!

Apple Brown Betty

3 lbs. cooking apples, cored,
   peeled and cut into eighths
10 slices bread, cubed
1/2 t. cinnamon
1/4 t. nutmeg
1/8 t. salt
3/4 c. brown sugar, packed
1/2 c. butter, melted
Garnish: whipped topping

Place apples in a slow cooker.
Combine remaining ingredients
except topping; toss together and
sprinkle over apples. Cover and
cook on low setting 2 to 4 hours.
Garnish with whipped topping.
Makes 6 to 8 servings.

193

Amy Crowe-Galloway
Pontotoc, MS

With a slow cooker, it's
so easy to make this yummy
old-fashioned favorite!

Easy Family-Style Corn

2 12-oz. pkgs. frozen corn
8-oz. pkg. cream cheese, cubed
1/4 c. butter, cubed
2 T. sugar
1 t. salt
1/2 t. pepper

Spray a slow cooker with non-stick vegetable spray. Add all ingredients; stir to combine. Cover and cook on low setting for 4 hours, stirring halfway through. Makes 8 to 10 servings.

Katie Dick
Olathe, KS

This is a scrumptious side for any main dish... tote it to a potluck right in the crock.

Sloppy Joe Chicken

6 skinless chicken thighs
8-oz. can tomato sauce
1-1/2 oz. pkg. Sloppy Joe mix
2 T. honey
cooked rice

Place chicken in a slow cooker.
Combine remaining ingredients
except rice; pour over chicken. Cover
and cook on low setting for 6 hours.
Discard bones. Serve chicken and
sauce over cooked rice. Serves 4.

195

Kathi Downey
Lompoc, CA

Super for any game-day
meal...it cooks up while
you're waiting for
the next touchdown!

Slow-Cooker Cola Ham

3 to 4-lb. fully cooked ham
1/2 c. brown sugar, packed
1 t. dry mustard
12-oz. can cola

Place ham in a slow cooker. Combine brown sugar and mustard; stir in enough cola to make a glaze consistency. Pour glaze over ham, coating well. Cover and cook on low setting for 8 to 10 hours, basting occasionally with juices. Serves 8 to 10.

Elsie Mellinger
Annville, PA

Baking a ham basted with cola produces a delicious gravy...guests will never guess your secret!

Scalloped Pineapple

1 c. sugar
3 eggs, beaten
3/4 c. butter, melted
3/4 c. milk
20-oz. can crushed pineapple,
   drained
8 slices bread, cubed
Garnish: vanilla ice cream

Mix all ingredients except ice cream
in a slow cooker. Cover and cook
on high for 2 hours. Reduce heat to
low; cook for one additional hour.
Garnish portions with scoops of
ice cream. Makes 8 servings.

197

Carol Smith
West Lawn, PA

It isn't a potluck to us
until someone brings the
Scalloped Pineapple! It's
so good with ice cream.

Calico Beans

2 lbs. ground beef, browned
   and drained
1/2 to 1 lb. bacon, crisply cooked
   and crumbled
1 onion, chopped
3 15-oz. cans pork & beans
2 16-oz. cans kidney beans
2 16-oz. cans baby butter beans
16-oz. can navy beans
1 c. catsup
1/2 c. brown sugar, packed
2 T. prepared horseradish
2 T. Worcestershire sauce
hot pepper sauce to taste

Add all ingredients to a slow cooker;
do not drain beans. Mix well. Cover
and cook on low setting for 6 hours.
Stir again before serving. Serves 20.

Judy Schlosser
Shubert, NE

This is an old family
favorite, requested
at all of our
family reunions.

Southern Pork Barbecue

Vicki Chavis
Fort Myers, FL

My whole family loves
this recipe and my friends
ask for it by name. It's
a great way to serve
a picnic crowd.

3-lb. boneless pork loin roast,
   trimmed
1 c. water
18-oz. bottle barbecue sauce
2 T. Worcestershire sauce
1 to 2 T. hot pepper sauce
1/4 c. brown sugar, packed
1 t. salt
1 t. pepper
16 to 20 mini hamburger
   buns, split

Place roast in a slow cooker; add
water. Cover and cook on high
setting for 7 hours. Shred meat;
return to slow cooker. Stir in
remaining ingredients; cover and
cook on low setting for one hour.
Serve on buns, topped with coleslaw.
Makes 8 to 10 servings, 2 buns each.

Coleslaw:

1 head cabbage, shredded
3 carrots, peeled and shredded
1 c. mayonnaise
1/3 c. sugar
1/4 c. cider vinegar

Combine cabbage and carrots. Blend
remaining ingredients; toss with
cabbage mixture. Makes 10 servings.

199

Mock Pierogies

1/2 c. butter, melted
1 c. onion, chopped
6 to 7 potatoes, peeled, cubed
  and cooked
16-oz. pkg. shredded Cheddar
  cheese, divided
16-oz. pkg. bowtie pasta, cooked

Combine butter and onion in a slow
cooker; add potatoes. Sprinkle with
half the cheese. Spread pasta on top;
sprinkle with remaining cheese. Cover
and cook on low setting for 30 to
40 minutes, stirring occasionally.
Serves 6 to 8.

**Kelly Ziemba
Port Saint Lucie, FL**

This wonderful, flavorful
casserole tastes just
like potato and cheese
pierogies...without
all the fuss!

Hot Spicy Cider for a Crowd

1 gal. apple cider
1 c. sugar
2 t. ground cloves
2 t. allspice
2 4-inch cinnamon sticks
1/4 c. orange juice
Optional: apple wedges

Combine all ingredients except apples in a slow cooker. Cover and cook on low setting for 5 to 6 hours, or on high setting for 2 to 3 hours. Discard cinnamon sticks before serving. If desired, garnish individual servings with apple wedges. Makes about 16 cups.

201

Edith Bolstad
Beaver Dam, WI

A crock-full of hot cider to sip...your secret to keeping warm on blustery days.

Deliciously Cheesy Potatoes

32-oz. pkg. frozen southern-style
hashbrowns, thawed
2 10-3/4 oz. cans Cheddar cheese
soup
2 12-oz. cans evaporated milk
2 2.8-oz. cans French fried
onions, divided

Combine all ingredients except onions.
Place half of mixture in a slow cooker;
top with one can of onions. Add
remaining potato mixture; top with
remaining onions. Cover and cook on
low setting for 8 hours, stirring
occasionally. Serves 8 to 10.

Cathy Jepson
Salida, CA

This recipe has been in
our family for many years.
It's always requested
by our children at
family gatherings.

Pork Sandwich Spread

2 to 3-lb. pork roast
1/4 t. dried basil
1/4 t. dried oregano
salt and pepper to taste
3 eggs, beaten
1 sleeve round buttery crackers,
    crushed
4-oz. jar chopped pimentos,
    drained
1 green pepper, chopped
20 sandwich buns, split
    and warmed

Place roast in a slow cooker; sprinkle with seasonings. Cover and cook on high setting for 2 to 3 hours, until fork-tender. Remove roast; cool. Reserve 1/2 cup cooking liquid. Grind roast with a meat grinder. Add remaining ingredients except buns, reserved liquid and enough water to obtain consistency of thick soup. Return mixture to slow cooker and cook on low setting for an additional 2 hours. Spoon onto buns. Makes 20 sandwiches.

Janie Reed
Zanesville, OH

This simple recipe helped my mom feed our large family. It was always a welcome meal on a cold winter day.

Special Beef Fajitas

1-1/2 lbs. beef round steak
14-1/2 oz. can diced tomatoes,
   drained
1 onion, sliced
1 green pepper, sliced into strips
1 red pepper, sliced into strips
1 jalapeño, chopped
2 cloves garlic, minced
1 t. fresh cilantro, chopped
1 t. chili powder
1 t. ground cumin
1 t. ground coriander
1/4 t. salt
8 to 10 6-inch flour tortillas
Garnish: sour cream, guacamole,
   salsa, shredded Cheddar cheese,
   shredded lettuce

Place beef in a slow cooker. Combine
vegetables and seasonings; spoon over
beef. Cover and cook on low setting
for 8 to 10 hours, or on high setting
for 4 to 5 hours. Shred beef; serve
with a slotted spoon on tortillas. Add
favorite toppings; roll up tortillas.
Makes 8 to 10 servings.

Erin Neuhaus
Lincoln, NE

These are always a
favorite for casual dinner
parties...the slow cooker
does all the work!

Spaghetti Sauce for a Crowd

28-oz. can crushed tomatoes
15-oz. can tomato sauce
12-oz. can tomato paste
1/2 c. onion, chopped
2 cloves garlic, minced
3 T. sugar
1 t. dried basil
1 t. dried oregano
1/2 t. salt
20-oz. pkg. Italian pork sausages,
    browned, drained and sliced
2 16-oz. pkgs. spaghetti,
    cooked

205

Stir together all ingredients except
sausages and spaghetti in a slow
cooker. Add sausages; cover and cook
on low for 8 hours. Serve sauce over
cooked spaghetti. Serves 12 to 14.

Kathie Lorenzini
Ignacio, CO

This is my daughter
Kerrie's recipe...we
think it's the best!

Warm Fruity Punch

32-oz. bottle cranberry juice
    cocktail
32-oz. can pineapple juice
1/3 c. red cinnamon candies
4-inch cinnamon stick
Optional: additional cinnamon
    sticks

Combine juices, candies and cinnamon
stick in a slow cooker. Cover and cook
on low setting for 2 to 5 hours. Remove
cinnamon stick before serving. Use
additional cinnamon sticks as stirrers,
if desired. Makes 8 servings.

Virginia Watson
Scranton, PA

Serve up mugs of this warm-
you-up punch after a family
outing in the frosty air.

Triple Chocolate Cake

18-1/2 oz. pkg. chocolate
    cake mix
8-oz. container sour cream
3.9-oz. pkg. instant chocolate
    pudding mix
12-oz. pkg. semi-sweet
    chocolate chips
4 eggs, beaten
3/4 c. oil
1 c. water
Garnish: vanilla ice cream

Place all ingredients except ice
cream in a slow cooker; mix well.
Cover and cook on high setting
for 3 to 4 hours. Serve warm,
garnished with scoops of ice cream.
Makes 8 to 10 servings.

207

Joan Brochu
Harwich, MA

This ooey-gooey dessert
is a chocolate
lover's delight!

Harvest Pecan Sweet Potatoes

2 29-oz. cans sweet potatoes,
  drained
1/3 c. plus 2 t. butter, melted
  and divided
2 T. sugar
1/3 c. plus 2 T. brown sugar,
  packed and divided
1 T. orange juice
2 eggs, beaten
1/2 c. milk
1/3 c. chopped pecans
2 T. all-purpose flour

Mash sweet potatoes in a large bowl;
blend in 1/3 cup melted butter, sugar
and 2 tablespoons brown sugar. Beat
in juice, eggs and milk; spoon into a
lightly greased slow cooker and set
aside. Combine pecans, flour,
remaining brown sugar and remaining
butter. Spread mixture over sweet
potatoes; cover and cook on high
setting for 3 to 4 hours. Makes 8 to
10 servings.

Nancy Girard
Chesapeake, VA

A delicious addition to
a holiday meal...I always
get lots of compliments!

Spoon Bread Florentine

10-oz. pkg. frozen chopped
    spinach, thawed and drained
6 green onions, sliced
1 red pepper, chopped
5-1/2 oz. pkg. cornbread mix
4 eggs, beaten
1/2 c. butter, melted
1 c. cottage cheese
1-1/4 t. seasoned salt

Combine all ingredients in a large
bowl; mix well. Spoon into a lightly
greased slow cooker. Cover, with
lid slightly ajar to allow moisture
to escape. Cook on low setting for
3 to 4 hours, or on high setting for
1-3/4 to 2 hours, until edges are
golden and a knife tip inserted in
center tests clean. Makes 8 servings.

209

Jo Ann
A deliciously different
side that's so simple
to make.

Joan's Chicken Stuffing Casserole

12-oz. pkg. chicken stuffing mix
3 10-3/4 oz. cans cream of chicken
   soup, divided
1/2 c. milk
3 to 4 c. cooked chicken, cubed
12-oz. pkg. shredded Cheddar
   cheese

Prepare stuffing mix according to
package directions; place in a slow
cooker. Stir in 2 cans soup. In a
separate bowl, stir together remaining
soup, milk and chicken. Add to slow
cooker. Spread cheese over top.
Cover and cook on low setting for
4 to 6 hours, or on high setting for
2 to 3 hours. Serves 6.

Joan Brochu
Harwich, MA
Hearty and so filling,
this chicken dish will
be the first to disappear
at any potluck.

Kielbasa & Red Beans

1 lb. Kielbasa, cut into
   bite-size pieces
4 to 5 16-oz. cans red beans,
   drained and rinsed
2 14-1/2 oz. cans diced tomatoes
1 onion, chopped
hot pepper sauce to taste

Combine all ingredients in a slow
cooker. Cover and cook on low
setting for 8 hours, or on high
setting for 4 to 5 hours.
Serves 6 to 8.

211

Beth Schlieper
Lakewood, CO

Serve over bowls of
rice for traditional
red beans & rice.

Easy Chili Rellenos

2 t. butter
7-oz. can whole green chiles,
   drained and cut in strips
8-oz. pkg. shredded Cheddar
   cheese
8-oz. pkg. shredded Monterey
   Jack cheese
14-1/2 oz. can stewed tomatoes
4 eggs, beaten
2 T. all-purpose flour
3/4 c. evaporated milk

Spread butter in a slow cooker. Layer
chiles and cheeses; add tomatoes. Stir
together eggs, flour and milk; pour
into slow cooker. Cover and cook on
high setting for 2 to 3 hours. Serves 6.

Betty Kozlowski
Newnan, GA

My husband fell in love
with this the first time
he tasted it! It's a
potluck pleaser too.

7-Spice Sticky Chicken

3-lb. chicken
1 t. salt
2 t. paprika
1 t. cayenne pepper
1 t. onion powder
1 t. dried thyme
1 t. white pepper
1/2 t. pepper
1/2 t. garlic powder
1 c. onion, chopped
cooked rice

213

Pat chicken dry with paper towels. Combine spices in a small bowl; mix well. Rub spice mixture well into chicken, inside and out. Place chicken in a large plastic zipping bag; refrigerate overnight. In the morning, place chicken in a slow cooker; top with onion. Cover and cook on low setting for 8 to 10 hours. Serve over cooked rice. Serves 4 to 6.

**Samantha Sparks
Madison, WI**

This is so tender and good...pass the napkins, please!

Staycation Coconut–Lime Bars, page 299

Giant Chocolate Malt Cookies, page 254

Chocolate Zucchini Cupcakes, page 235

Iced Raspberry Delights, page 293

101 CUPCAKE, COOKIE & BROWNIE *Recipes*

Pistachio Thumbprints, page 253

Breezy Kite Cupcakes, page 225

The Best Blondies, page 295

Add a sweet ending to every meal with this collection of delicious confections…sweet & simple cupcakes, classic cookies and mouth-watering brownies & bars.

Chocolate-Orange Snowballs, page 271

Swirled Peanut Butter
Cheesecake Bars, page 288

Easiest Boston Cream Cupcakes, page 233

Baking
TIPS

★ Oven temperatures can vary, so test for doneness after the minimum baking time.

★ Bake up the best texture for brownies and bars...use a wooden spoon to mix in dry ingredients just until moistened.

★ For evenly baked and uniform cupcakes, fill liners about 2/3 full, using an ice cream scoop or measuring cup.

★ Before adding the batter for bar cookies or brownies, mold aluminum foil over the bottom of the baking pan, then pop the pre-formed foil inside.

★ Turn any cupcake recipe into minis...just decrease the baking time by 5 to 7 minutes.

★ If baked cookies are difficult to remove from the baking sheet, reheat the sheet in the oven for one minute, then remove.

★ Keep cookie dough from spreading by cooling baking sheets between batches.

★ Make sure goodies are completely cooled before decorating. Gently brush off any crumbs with a pastry brush or your fingers.

★ Cut brownies and bars smoothly and easily! First, place the pan in the freezer for several minutes. For each cut, dip a plastic knife in hot water, wipe it dry, and move it across the pan in an up-and-down sawing motion.

Orange Puff Cupcakes

1/3 c. margarine
1 c. sugar
2 eggs, beaten
1-3/4 c. all-purpose flour
1 T. baking powder
1/2 c. frozen orange juice
    concentrate, thawed
Optional: zest of 1 orange
Garnish: white frosting, orange
    zest strips

Beat together margarine and sugar
in a bowl; add eggs. Combine flour
and baking powder; add alternately
with orange juice to margarine
mixture. Stir in zest, if using. Fill
paper-lined muffin cups 2/3 full.
Bake at 375 degrees for 15 minutes.
Let cool. Spread with frosting and
garnish with orange zest strips, if
desired. Makes one dozen.

217

Heather Roberts
Quebec, Canada

This is an old-fashioned
recipe handed down from my
grandmother. The ladies at
our annual church social
recommend this recipe for
our bake sale and tea table.

Cream Cheese-Filled Cupcakes

18-1/4 oz. pkg. German chocolate
  cake mix
1 c. mini semi-sweet chocolate
  chips
1/3 c. sugar
1 egg, beaten
8-oz. pkg. cream cheese, softened

Prepare cake mix according to package directions. Fill paper-lined muffin cups 1/2 full. Combine remaining ingredients; drop by teaspoonfuls onto batter. Bake at 350 degrees for 20 to 25 minutes. Cool completely. Makes about 2 dozen.

Melissa Mishler
Columbia City, IN

These are so delicious,
you might want to make
a double batch!

Grandma's Banana Cupcakes

1/2 c. butter, softened
1-3/4 c. sugar
2 eggs, beaten
2 c. all-purpose flour
1 t. baking soda
1 t. baking powder
1 c. sour milk
2 bananas, mashed
1 t. vanilla extract
1/2 c. chopped pecans
Garnish: Cream Cheese Frosting
    (found on page 33),
    banana slices
Optional: caramel sauce

219

Blend butter for 5 minutes, using an electric mixer on medium speed. Slowly add sugar; beat in eggs. Combine flour, baking soda and baking powder; add to butter mixture alternately with milk. Stir in bananas, vanilla and pecans. Fill paper-lined muffin cups 1/2 full. Bake at 350 degrees for 18 to 25 minutes, until a toothpick inserted in the center comes out clean. Allow to cool; frost with Cream Cheese Frosting and drizzle with caramel sauce, if using. Top with banana slices. Keep refrigerated. Makes 1-1/2 to 2 dozen.

Kelly Marcum
Rock Falls, IL

My grandma made these often...so yummy! To make sour milk, stir one teaspoon of white vinegar into one cup of milk and let stand for 5 minutes.

2-Kiss Cupcakes

3/4 c. butter, softened
1-2/3 c. sugar
3 eggs, beaten
1-1/2 t. vanilla extract
2 c. all-purpose flour
2/3 c. baking cocoa
1-1/4 t. baking soda
1/4 t. baking powder
1 t. salt
1-1/3 c. water
60 milk chocolate drops, divided

Beat butter, sugar, eggs and vanilla; set aside. Combine flour, cocoa, baking soda, baking powder and salt; add alternately with water to butter mixture. Fill paper-lined muffin cups half full. Place a chocolate drop in center of each. Bake at 350 degrees for 20 minutes. Let cool. Frost with Chocolate Frosting. Top each with a chocolate drop. Makes 2-1/2 dozen.

Chocolate Frosting:

1/4 c. margarine, melted
1/2 c. baking cocoa
1/3 c. milk
1 t. vanilla extract
3-1/2 c. powdered sugar

Combine all ingredients; beat until smooth.

Athena Colegrove
Big Springs, TX
Bake these for your family and you'll be guaranteed not just kisses, but several hugs, too!

Key Lime Cupcakes

16-oz. pkg. angel food cake mix
3/4 c. lemon-lime soda
1/2 c. plus 1 T. key lime juice,
  divided
14-oz. can sweetened condensed
  milk
1 t. lime zest
8-oz. container frozen whipped
  topping, thawed
Garnish: sweetened flaked
  coconut

In a large bowl, combine dry cake mix, soda and 1/4 cup key lime juice. Spray muffin cups with non-stick vegetable spray. Fill muffin cups 2/3 full. Bake at 350 degrees for 12 minutes, or until a toothpick tests clean. Cool completely. Use a toothpick to poke several holes almost to the bottom of each cupcake; don't poke through bottoms. Mix together remaining lime juice, sweetened condensed milk and lime zest. Measure out 1/3 cup lime mixture; pour over all the cupcake tops. Stir whipped topping into the remaining lime mixture; chill for one hour. Frost cupcakes with whipped topping mixture. Garnish with coconut. Refrigerate until serving time. Makes 2 dozen.

221

Lena Smith
Pickerington, OH
I spent the summer trying different-flavored cupcakes. I made these for our church's bake-off and won Honorable Mention!

Pineapple Upside-Down Cupcakes

20-oz. can pineapple chunks,
    drained and 1/2 c. juice reserved
1/3 c. brown sugar, packed
1/3 c. butter, melted
1 c. all-purpose flour
3/4 c. sugar
1/2 t. baking powder
1/4 c. butter, softened
1 egg, beaten
Garnish: maraschino cherries

Pat pineapple dry with paper towels.
In a bowl, combine brown sugar and
melted butter; divide evenly into
12 greased muffin cups. Arrange
pineapple chunks over brown sugar
mixture. In a bowl, combine flour,
sugar and baking powder. Mix in
softened butter and reserved pineapple
juice; beat for 2 minutes. Beat in egg.
Spoon batter over pineapple, filling
each cup 3/4 full. Bake at 350 degrees
for 30 minutes, or until a toothpick
tests clean. Cool in pan for 5 minutes.
Place a wire rack on top of muffin tin
and invert cupcakes onto rack so
pineapple is on top. Cool completely
and top each with a cherry. Makes
one dozen.

Sharon Tillman
Hampton, VA

When I was little, every
spring my Grandma Bernadean
would invite me for a tea
party with lemonade and
these cupcakes!

Whoopie Cupcakes

1-1/2 c. all-purpose flour
1 c. sugar
1 t. baking soda
1 t. salt
1/3 c. plus 1 T. baking cocoa
3 T. shortening
4 t. vinegar
1 c. milk
1 t. vanilla extract
Garnish: powdered sugar

Combine flour, sugar, baking soda, salt and cocoa. Add shortening, vinegar, milk and vanilla. Beat for 2 minutes. Fill greased muffin cups 2/3 full. Bake at 350 degrees for 20 to 25 minutes. Cool. Cut off tops in an inverted cone shape so it narrows toward the center of the cakes. Fill cupcakes with filling and replace tops; sprinkle with powdered sugar. Makes one dozen.

Filling:

3/4 c. margarine
3/4 c. shortening
1-1/2 c. sugar
4-1/2 t. all-purpose flour
1/8 t. salt
3/4 c. milk, room temperature
1 T. vanilla extract

Beat all ingredients for 8 minutes with an electric mixer, or until fluffy.

223

Janie Corliss
Front Royal, VA

I began making these cupcakes when my sons were babies. They're so much easier to make than whoopie pies and taste just as good!

Special Mocha Cupcakes

Barbara Humiston
Tampa, FL

Invite your best girlfriend over for conversation, a mug of coffee and a cupcake...or two!

1-1/2 c. all-purpose flour
1 c. sugar
1/3 c. baking cocoa
1 t. baking soda
1/2 t. salt
2 eggs, beaten
1/2 c. brewed coffee, chilled
1/2 c. oil
1 T. vinegar
1 T. vanilla extract

Combine flour, sugar, cocoa, baking soda and salt; set aside. Combine remaining ingredients; add to flour mixture and stir well. Fill paper-lined muffin cups 2/3 full. Bake at 350 degrees for 20 to 25 minutes. Cool in tin on wire rack for 10 minutes. Remove from tin; cool completely. Frost with Mocha Frosting. Makes one dozen.

Mocha Frosting:

3 T. semi-sweet chocolate chips, melted
3 T. milk chocolate chips, melted
1/3 c. butter, softened
2 c. powdered sugar
1 to 2 T. brewed coffee, chilled

Combine chocolate and butter; gradually beat in powdered sugar. Stir in coffee until smooth.

Breezy Kite Cupcakes

18-1/4 oz. pkg. chocolate
   cake mix
1-1/2 c. candy-coated chocolate
   mini-baking bits, divided
24 graham cracker squares
16-oz. container white frosting,
   divided
assorted food colorings

Prepare cake mix according to package instructions. Fill paper-lined muffin cups 2/3 full; sprinkle each with one teaspoon baking bits. Bake at 350 degrees for 20 to 25 minutes; cool completely on wire racks. Using a serrated knife, gently cut graham cracker squares into kite shapes; set aside. Tint half the frosting blue; tint remaining frosting desired kite colors. Frost cupcakes with blue frosting; frost graham kites with remaining frostings as desired. Tilt cracker slightly and arrange on cupcake top. Add a string tail of mini-baking bits. Makes 2 dozen.

225

Penny Sherman
Cumming, GA

On a rainy day, spirits are bound to lift when you serve these pretty cakes!

Chocolate & Marshmallow Cupcakes

8-oz. pkg. unsweetened dark
    baking chocolate, chopped
1 c. butter, softened
4 eggs
1 c. sugar
3/4 c. all-purpose flour
1 t. salt
1/2 c. mini semi-sweet chocolate
    chips
Garnish: 1/2 c. mini marshmallows

Place chocolate and butter together in a microwave-safe bowl; microwave on high setting just until melted. Cool slightly, just until warm. Blend together eggs and sugar until light and foamy. Add flour and salt; mix well. Pour in chocolate mixture; blend until smooth. Fill paper-lined muffin cups 2/3 full. Sprinkle one teaspoon chocolate chips over each cupcake. Bake at 350 degrees for 15 minutes, until a toothpick tests clean. Remove from oven; arrange several marshmallows on top of each cupcake. Broil just until marshmallows turn golden. Remove from oven and let stand 5 minutes to cool slightly. Makes one dozen.

Kathy Grashoff
Fort Wayne, IN

Drizzle with chocolate
or caramel sauce for a
divine delight!

Bears at the Beach

18-1/4 oz. pkg. favorite cake mix
16-oz. container white frosting
blue and yellow food coloring
24 bear-shaped graham crackers
Garnish: blue and yellow sugar
    sprinkles
24 peach ring jelly candies
6.6-oz. pkg. fruit-flavored snack
    rolls, cut into 24 2-inch
    pieces
Optional: paper parasols

Prepare cake mix and bake cupcakes according to package directions; let cool. Tint half the frosting with blue food coloring and frost half the cupcakes. Tint the remaining frosting with yellow food coloring and frost the remaining cupcakes. Sprinkle blue cupcakes with blue sprinkles and yellow cupcakes with yellow sprinkles. Lay a piece of snack roll onto each yellow cupcake and attach a graham cracker with a dot of icing. Insert a graham cracker through the center of each jelly candy and place on blue cupcakes. Insert paper parasols, if desired. Makes 2 dozen.

Dolores Adamo
Wallingford, CT
A cute dessert for summer picnics...so sweet!

Cheery Cherry Cupcakes

18-1/4 oz. pkg. chocolate cake mix
1-1/3 c. water
1/2 c. oil
3 eggs, beaten
21-oz. can cherry pie filling,
    divided
16-oz. container vanilla frosting

In a bowl, combine dry cake mix, water, oil and eggs. Spoon batter by 1/4 cupfuls into paper-lined muffin cups. Spoon a rounded teaspoon of pie filling onto the center of each cupcake. Bake at 350 degrees for 20 to 25 minutes, until a toothpick inserted on an angle toward the center tests clean. Cool completely in tins on wire racks. Frost cupcakes with vanilla frosting; top each with one cherry from pie filling. Makes 2 dozen.

**Tina Dillon
Parma, OH**

Whenever his birthday rolls around, my husband Terry starts dropping not-so-subtle hints about these sweet treats!

Taffy Apple Cupcakes ▶

18-1/4 oz. pkg. carrot cake mix
1 c. Granny Smith apples, cored,
    peeled and finely chopped
1/2 t. cinnamon
20 caramels, unwrapped
1/4 c. milk
1 c. pecans or walnuts, finely
    chopped
12 wooden craft sticks

Prepare cake mix according to package instructions; stir in apples and cinnamon. Fill paper-lined jumbo muffin cups 2/3 full. Bake at 350 degrees for 20 to 25 minutes, until a toothpick inserted near center tests clean. Combine caramels and milk in a small saucepan over low heat; stir until melted and smooth. Drizzle caramel over cooled cupcakes; sprinkle nuts over top. Insert a craft stick into center of each cupcake. Makes one dozen.

**Angie Biggins
Lyons, IL**

What fun...a gooey
caramel-topped cupcake
on a stick!

Cookie Dough Cupcakes

18-1/4 oz. pkg. yellow cake mix
1 c. milk
3 eggs, beaten
1/2 c. butter, melted and cooled
  slightly
1 t. vanilla extract
16-1/2 oz. tube refrigerated
  chocolate chip cookie dough
16-oz. container chocolate frosting
Garnish: 12 chocolate chip
  cookies, halved

In a bowl, combine dry cake mix, milk, eggs, butter and vanilla; beat for 2 minutes. Fill paper-lined muffin cups 1/3 full. Roll tablespoonfuls of cookie dough into balls. Place a ball into center of each cupcake. Top with remaining batter. Bake at 350 degrees for 15 to 20 minutes, until a toothpick tests clean. Cool in tin on wire racks 10 minutes. Remove from pan; cool completely. Frost with chocolate frosting. Garnish with cookie halves. Makes 2 dozen.

Jo Ann
Put the kids to work rolling the cookie dough into balls...and watch so they don't gobble up the cookies!

Hot Fudge Sundae Cupcakes

18-1/4 oz. pkg. devil's food
   cake mix
24 sugar cones
1-1/2 qt. vanilla ice cream
12-oz. jar hot fudge sauce
Garnish: whipped cream,
   peanuts, maraschino cherries

Prepare cake mix according to package directions. Fill paper-lined muffin cups 2/3 full. Bake at 350 degrees for 15 to 20 minutes. Cool completely on wire racks. For each cupcake, top with a scoop of ice cream, drizzle with hot fudge sauce and top with whipped cream. Place the cone into the whipped cream and sprinkle with peanuts and a cherry. Serve immediately. Makes 2 dozen.

231

Jennifer Licon-Conner
Gooseberry Patch

An impressive-looking
dessert that comes together
in a snap!

Almond Petit-Fours

18-1/4 oz. pkg. yellow cake mix
1/2 t. almond extract
3 c. sliced almonds
Garnish: candy-coated almonds

In a bowl, prepare cake mix according to package directions, adding almond extract into the batter. Fill paper-lined mini muffin cups 2/3 full. Bake at 350 degrees for 15 to 17 minutes; cool completely on wire racks. Spread Almond Frosting on half the cupcakes; these will be the bottom-layer cupcakes. Remove the liners from the remaining cupcakes and place them upside-down on top of the bottom-layer cupcakes. Frost the top-layer cupcakes on all sides. Coat cupcake sides with sliced almonds. Arrange candy-coated almonds on top. Makes about 3 dozen.

Almond Frosting:

3 c. powdered sugar
2 t. almond extract
3 T. hot water

In a bowl, combine all ingredients. Beat to desired consistency, adding more water or sugar as needed.

Jill Valentine
Jackson, TN
The trick to this elegant dessert is stacking mini cupcakes. Tint the frosting with food coloring or garnish with sprinkles for variety.

Easiest Boston Cream Cupcakes

18-1/4 oz. pkg. yellow cake mix
3.4-oz. pkg. instant vanilla
   pudding mix
1 c. cold milk
1-1/2 c. frozen whipped topping,
   thawed and divided
4 1-oz. sqs. semi-sweet baking
   chocolate

Prepare cake mix according to package directions. Fill greased muffin cups 2/3 full and bake at 350 degrees for 15 to 20 minutes. Cool completely. Whisk pudding mix and milk for 2 minutes; let stand 5 minutes. Use a serrated knife to cut off the top of each cupcake; set tops aside. Stir 1/2 cup whipped topping into pudding. Spoon one tablespoon onto each cupcake; replace cupcake tops. In a microwave-safe bowl, combine remaining whipped topping and chocolate. Microwave for one minute; stir and microwave an additional 30 seconds. Stir until chocolate is melted; let stand 15 minutes. Frost cupcakes with chocolate mixture. Makes 2 dozen.

Robin Hill
Rochester, NY
Our family is known to enjoy these cupcakes as an extra-special breakfast!

Double Maple Cupcakes

1/2 c. sugar
1/3 c. plus 2 T. butter, softened
  and divided
1-1/2 t. vanilla extract, divided
1-1/2 t. maple flavoring, divided
2 eggs, beaten
1-1/4 c. all-purpose flour
1-1/4 t. baking powder
1/4 t. plus 1/8 t. salt, divided
1/4 c. milk
1/4 c. plus 3 T. maple syrup,
  divided
1-3/4 c. powdered sugar

Blend sugar, 1/3 cup butter, one teaspoon vanilla and one teaspoon maple flavoring. Beat in eggs. In another bowl, mix flour, baking powder and 1/4 teaspoon salt. In a third bowl, blend milk and 1/4 cup syrup. Add flour mixture and syrup mixture alternately into sugar mixture. Divide batter among 12 paper-lined muffin cups. Bake at 350 degrees for 20 to 25 minutes. Cool in tin 10 minutes; cool completely on wire racks. For the frosting, combine remaining 3 tablespoons syrup, 2 tablespoons butter, 1/2 teaspoon vanilla, 1/2 teaspoon maple flavoring and 1/8 teaspoon salt until fluffy. Gradually blend in powdered sugar. Frost cupcakes. Makes one dozen.

Gail Prather
Hastings, NE

I love using the fresh maple syrup I get at our local farmers' market for these cupcakes...it gives them such a nice flavor.

Chocolate Zucchini Cupcakes

2 c. zucchini, shredded
3 eggs, beaten
2 c. sugar
3/4 c. oil
2 t. vanilla extract
2 c. all-purpose flour
2/3 c. baking cocoa
1/2 t. baking powder
1 t. baking soda
1 t. salt
3/4 c. milk chocolate chips

Combine zucchini, eggs, sugar, oil and vanilla. Add flour, cocoa, baking powder, baking soda and salt; stir in chocolate chips. Fill paper-lined muffin cups 2/3 full. Bake at 325 degrees for 25 minutes, or until a toothpick inserted near center tests clean. Cool in tin 5 minutes. Remove from tin; cool completely. Frost with Peanut Butter Frosting. Makes 2 dozen.

Peanut Butter Frosting:

1/2 c. creamy peanut butter
1/3 c. butter, softened
1 T. milk
1/2 t. vanilla extract
1-1/2 c. powdered sugar

Beat peanut butter, butter, milk and vanilla until smooth. Gradually beat in powdered sugar.

235

Michelle Rooney
Sunbury, OH
So moist and delicious...no one will guess the secret ingredient is zucchini!

Yummy Spice Cupcakes

2 c. all-purpose flour
1 t. baking soda
1/2 t. baking powder
1/2 t. cinnamon
1 t. pumpkin pie spice
1/2 t. salt
1 c. sugar
1/2 c. butter, melted
15-oz. jar applesauce
Optional: 1/2 c. raisins

In a bowl, combine flour, baking soda, baking powder and spices. Stir in sugar and butter. Mix in applesauce until well combined. Stir in raisins, if using. Fill greased muffin cups 2/3 full. Bake at 350 degrees for 20 to 25 minutes, until a toothpick tests clean. Cool completely. Frost with Vanilla Butter Cream Frosting. Makes 1-1/2 dozen.

Vanilla Butter Cream Frosting:

1/2 c. butter, softened
4 c. powdered sugar
1/2 t. salt
1/3 c. milk
1 t. vanilla extract

In a large bowl, beat butter until smooth. Add remaining ingredients; mix until smooth and creamy.

Brenda Stocks
Preston, ID

If raisins aren't your favorite, try milk chocolate chips.

Pineapple-Orange Cakes

18-1/4 oz. pkg. pineapple
   cake mix
11-oz. can mandarin oranges
4 eggs, beaten
1/2 c. sour cream

In a large bowl, combine dry cake mix, oranges with juice, eggs and sour cream. Beat with an electric mixer on medium speed for 2 minutes. Fill greased muffin cups 2/3 full. Bake at 350 degrees for 20 minutes, or until a toothpick tests clean. Cool in tin on wire racks 5 minutes. Remove from tin and cool completely. Frost cupcakes with Orange Frosting. Refrigerate until ready to serve. Makes 2 dozen.

Orange Frosting:

4-oz. cream cheese, softened
1/4 c. butter, softened
1-1/2 t. orange zest
4-1/2 t. orange juice
3 c. powdered sugar

In a large bowl, beat cream cheese and butter with an electric mixer at medium speed until creamy. Beat in orange zest and juice until combined. Gradually beat in powdered sugar until smooth.

Michelle Campen
Peoria, IL
My friend made me these cupcakes...they were so good, I had to ask her for the recipe!

Strawberry Cupcake Cones

2 c. all-purpose flour
1/2 c. sugar
2 t. baking powder
1/2 t. baking soda
1/2 t. salt
2 eggs, beaten
6-oz. container whipped-style
   strawberry yogurt
1/2 c. oil
1/2 t. strawberry extract
1 c. strawberries, hulled and
   chopped
15 flat-bottomed ice cream cones
Optional: chocolate frosting
Garnish: sprinkles

Combine flour, sugar, baking powder, baking soda and salt. In another bowl, beat eggs, yogurt, oil, extract and strawberries. Stir egg mixture into flour mixture just until combined. Spoon 2 tablespoons batter into each cone. Place cones in ungreased muffin cups. Bake at 375 degrees for 18 to 20 minutes; let cool. Decorate with frosting or Chocolate Glaze; garnish as desired. Makes 15.

Chocolate Glaze:

1 c. semi-sweet chocolate chips
1 T. shortening

Melt ingredients together over low heat and stir until smooth.

Jackie Smulski
Lyons, IL

You don't have to worry about melting or spills with these cones. Sure to disappear fast!

Tiny Turtle Cupcakes

21-1/2 oz. pkg. brownie mix
1/2 c. pecans, chopped
16-oz. container dark chocolate
    fudge frosting
1/2 c. pecans, toasted and
    coarsely chopped

Prepare brownie batter according to package directions. Stir in chopped pecans. Fill paper-lined mini muffin cups 2/3 full. Bake at 350 degrees for 18 minutes, or until a toothpick tests clean. Cool cupcakes in tins on wire racks 5 minutes. Remove from tins; cool completely. Frost cupcakes; top with toasted pecans. Spoon Caramel Sauce evenly over cupcakes. Store in refrigerator. Makes 4-1/2 dozen.

Caramel Sauce:

12 caramels, unwrapped
1 to 2 T. whipping cream

Combine caramels and one tablespoon cream in a small saucepan; cook and stir over low heat until smooth. Add remaining cream as needed for desired consistency.

Teresa Podracky
Solon, OH
I give these little chocolate bites to my kids' soccer coaches for an end-of-the-season gift...and keep some for myself, too!

Mini Mousse Cupcakes

2-1/3 c. milk chocolate chips
6 eggs, beaten
1/4 c. plus 2 T. all-purpose flour
Garnish: whipped cream,
  chocolate shavings

Melt chocolate in a double boiler over medium heat and let cool slightly. In a large bowl, beat eggs and flour. Beat in melted chocolate until combined. Fill paper-lined mini muffin cups 2/3 full. Bake at 325 degrees for 7 to 10 minutes, until edges are done and centers shake slightly. Cool in tin on wire rack for 20 minutes. Remove from tin; cool completely. Garnish with whipped cream and chocolate shavings. Makes about 2 dozen.

Vickie
Chocolate lovers will swoon over these delectable cakes!

Sweet Angel Cupcakes

16-oz. pkg. angel food cake mix
2 T. poppy seed
1-1/2 t. almond extract, divided
1/2 c. sliced almonds, chopped
1-1/2 c. powdered sugar
1 T. plus 2 t. water

Prepare cake mix according to package directions, adding poppy seed and one teaspoon extract to batter. Fill paper-lined muffin cups 2/3 full. Sprinkle batter with almonds. Bake at 350 degrees for 15 to 20 minutes, until tops are golden. Let cool completely. Combine powdered sugar, water and remaining extract, stirring until smooth. Drizzle icing over cupcakes. Makes 2-1/2 dozen.

241

Roxanne Vilhauer
Springfield, MO
Put several cupcakes in a tea towel-lined basket with a note that reads, "You're an angel!" A sweet thank-you for a friend.

Snickerdoodle Cupcakes

18-1/4 oz. pkg. white cake mix
1 c. milk
1/2 c. butter, melted and cooled
  slightly
3 eggs, beaten
1 t. vanilla extract
2 t. cinnamon

In a large bowl, combine dry cake mix and remaining ingredients. Beat with an electric mixer on low speed for 3 minutes. Fill greased muffin cups 2/3 full. Bake at 350 degrees for 22 to 25 minutes. Let cool. Frost with Cinnamon Frosting. Makes 2 dozen.

Cinnamon Frosting:

1/2 c. butter, softened
1 t. vanilla extract
1 T. cinnamon
3-3/4 c. powdered sugar
3 to 4 T. milk

Beat butter until fluffy. Mix in vanilla, cinnamon and powdered sugar. Stir in enough milk for desired consistency.

Diana Bulls
Reedley, CA

An easy and delicious version of an all-time favorite cookie!

Lemonade Cupcakes

1/2 c. frozen lemonade
   concentrate, thawed
18-1/4 oz. pkg. white cake mix
8-oz. container sour cream
3-oz. pkg. cream cheese, softened
3 eggs, beaten
2 T. lemon zest
Optional: lemon drops

In a bowl, combine all ingredients
except lemon drops. Beat with an
electric mixer on low speed for
3 minutes. Fill paper-lined muffin
cups 2/3 full. Bake at 350 degrees
for 22 minutes, or until a toothpick
tests clean. Frost with Cream Cheese
Frosting; garnish with lemon drops,
if desired. Makes 2-1/2 dozen.

Cream Cheese Frosting:

8-oz. pkg. cream cheese,
   softened
1/2 c. butter, softened
2 t. vanilla extract
16-oz. pkg. powdered sugar

Beat together cream cheese and
butter until smooth. Blend in vanilla.
Gradually beat in powdered sugar.

Sandy Roy
Crestwood, KY

Offer these little cakes
at your lemonade stand
and watch the customers
line up!

Toasted Coconut Cupcakes

9-oz. pkg. white cake mix
1/2 c. milk
1 egg white
1 t. vanilla
1 t. cinnamon

Combine all ingredients in a bowl. Beat with an electric mixer on medium speed until combined, about 2 minutes. Fill paper-lined muffin cups half full. Bake at 350 degrees for 20 to 25 minutes. Let cool slightly. While cupcakes are warm in the tin, spread 2 teaspoons Coconut Frosting onto the center of each; don't spread to edges. Broil cupcakes in tin until coconut is lightly toasted, about 2 to 3 minutes. Makes one dozen.

Coconut Frosting:

1/4 c. butter, softened
1/3 c. brown sugar, packed
2 T. milk
1 c. sweetened flaked coconut
1 t. cinnamon

Combine butter and brown sugar. Blend in remaining ingredients.

Kerry Mayer
Dunham Springs, LA
My sister, Vanessa, made these amazing cupcakes for a church bake sale and they were a tremendous success.

Peanut Butter Cup Cupcakes

1/3 c. butter, softened
1/3 c. creamy peanut butter
1-1/4 c. brown sugar, packed
2 eggs, beaten
1 t. vanilla extract
1-3/4 c. all-purpose flour
1-3/4 t. baking powder
1 t. salt
1 c. milk
16 mini peanut butter cups

In a bowl, combine butter, peanut butter and brown sugar. Beat in eggs and vanilla. Combine flour, baking powder and salt; add to butter mixture alternately with milk. Fill paper-lined muffin cups half full. Press a peanut butter cup into the center of each, until top edge is even with batter. Bake at 350 degrees for 22 to 24 minutes, until a toothpick inserted on an angle toward the center tests clean. Cool in tin on wire rack 10 minutes. Remove from tin and cool completely. Makes 16.

245

Kathy Murphy
Lawrence, NE

I serve these at Sunday morning coffee time at church. There are never any leftovers!

Madelene's Buttermilk-Molasses Cookies

1-1/2 c. sugar, divided
1 c. shortening
1 c. light molasses
1 c. buttermilk
1 t. vanilla extract
5 c. all-purpose flour
4 t. baking soda
1/2 t. salt
1/2 t. ground ginger
1/2 t. cinnamon
Optional: 1 c. raisins

In a bowl, beat together one cup sugar, shortening, molasses, buttermilk and vanilla. In another bowl, combine flour, baking soda, salt and spices. Stir flour mixture into sugar mixture; mix in raisins, if desired. Drop by rounded teaspoonfuls 2 inches apart on greased baking sheets. Sprinkle with remaining sugar to cover. Bake at 350 degrees for 12 to 15 minutes. Makes 2 to 3 dozen.

Casey Tabolt
Pulaski, NY

My grandmother would make these cookies and then call our house. We went right over so we could eat them warm out of the oven!

Iced Carrot Cookies

1 c. butter, softened
3/4 c. sugar
1 egg, beaten
1 c. carrot, peeled, cooked
   and mashed
2 c. all-purpose flour
2 t. baking powder
1/2 t. salt
1 t. vanilla extract
3 to 4 drops almond extract

Blend together butter and sugar; add egg and carrots. In a separate bowl, sift together flour, baking powder and salt; add to butter mixture, blending well. Stir in extracts. Drop by teaspoonfuls onto greased baking sheets. Bake at 375 degrees for 10 minutes, or until just lightly golden. Let cool and frost with Citrus Icing. Makes 3 dozen.

Citrus Icing:

1/4 c. butter, softened
2 c. powdered sugar
3 T. orange or lemon juice
1 T. orange or lemon zest

Blend butter and powdered sugar. Add juice and zest; mix well.

247

Paula Purcell
Plymouth Meeting, PA
One of my daughter's favorite stories was *Rabbit Finds a Way*, about a bunny who loved goodies made with carrots. Erin wanted these cookies whenever we read the story!

Double Chocolate Cookies

1 c. sugar
1 c. brown sugar, packed
1 c. butter, softened
2 eggs, beaten
1 t. baking soda
1 t. cream of tartar
1/2 t. salt
2 c. all-purpose flour
1/2 c. baking cocoa
1 c. semi-sweet chocolate chips
Garnish: additional sugar

In a large bowl, mix sugar, brown
sugar, butter and eggs. In another
bowl, whisk remaining ingredients
except chocolate chips and garnish.
Add flour mixture to sugar mixture
and combine until well blended. Stir
in chocolate chips. Form dough into
one-inch balls; roll in additional sugar.
Place on ungreased baking sheets. Bake
at 350 degrees for 8 to 10 minutes.
Makes 3 dozen.

Kristi Watson
Highland Ranch, CO

Doubly delectable!
For variety, use white
chocolate chips.

Tasty Cookie Pops

Claire Bertram
Lexington, KY
Ever since I discovered
these pops, I've been
making them for every
special occasion!

1/2 c. butter, softened
1/2 c. shortening
1 c. sugar
1 c. powdered sugar
2 eggs, beaten
3/4 c. oil
2 t. vanilla extract
4 c. all-purpose flour
1 t. baking soda
1 t. salt
1 t. cream of tartar
Garnish: sprinkles
lollipop sticks

249

Beat butter and shortening until
fluffy; add sugars, beating well.
Beat in eggs, oil and vanilla. In a
separate bowl, combine flour and
remaining ingredients except
sprinkles. Add flour mixture to
butter mixture, blending well. Cover
and chill 2 hours. Shape dough into
1-1/2 inch balls. Roll each ball in
sprinkles, pressing gently, if needed,
to coat. Place 2 inches apart on
ungreased baking sheets. Insert a
stick about one inch into each ball.
Bake at 350 degrees for 10 to
11 minutes, until set. Let cool
2 minutes on baking sheets; cool
completely on wire racks. Makes
4-1/2 dozen.

Brown Sugar-Apple Cookies

1 c. brown sugar, packed
2 eggs, beaten
1/2 t. baking soda
1 t. cinnamon
1/2 t. salt
1/2 c. shortening
2 t. vanilla extract
2 c. all-purpose flour
1 c. apples, cored, peeled and
    sliced

Mix together all ingredients, stirring in apples last. Drop by teaspoonfuls onto ungreased baking sheets. Bake at 350 degrees for 8 to 10 minutes. Makes 3-1/2 to 4 dozen.

Nancy Hannon
Lewistown, PA

Perfect for sharing with friends over a steamy pot of spiced tea.

Winslow Whoopie Pies

1/3 c. baking cocoa
1 c. sugar
1 egg, beaten
1/3 c. shortening, melted and
   cooled
3/4 c. milk
2 c. all-purpose flour
1 t. baking soda
1/8 t. salt
1 t. vanilla extract
Optional: chocolate sprinkles

In a bowl, combine cocoa and sugar. In another bowl, beat egg and shortening; add to cocoa mixture and stir in remaining ingredients except sprinkles. Drop by rounded tablespoonfuls onto lightly greased baking sheets. Bake at 350 degrees for 15 minutes. Let cool. Frost the flat sides of half the cookies with Marshmallow Filling; top with remaining cookies. Roll edges in sprinkles, if using. Makes one dozen.

Marshmallow Filling:

2 c. powdered sugar
2/3 c. shortening
2 T. milk
6 T. marshmallow creme
1 t. vanilla extract

Combine all ingredients; stir until smooth.

Carissa Ellerd
Thomaston, ME

This yummy and often-requested family recipe is a huge hit at any social gathering. I like to tint the filling with food coloring to match the occasion!

Oh-So-Fun Fortune Cookies

Your baking talents win the applause of others.

Karen Ensign
Providence, UT

These are the best-tasting fortune cookies! I add in jokes or fun fortunes and give them out as gifts... people love them!

3 egg whites, beaten
3/4 c. sugar
1/8 t. salt
1/4 c. canola oil
1/2 t. vanilla extract
1/2 t. almond extract
1 T. water
1 c. all-purpose flour
3-inch by 1/2-inch paper fortunes

Mix egg whites, sugar and salt. Add remaining ingredients except fortunes; mix thoroughly. Batter will be very thin. Make 2 cookies at a time, otherwise, the cookies will harden before you can shape them. Spray parchment paper-lined baking sheets with non-stick vegetable spray. Spread batter by teaspoonfuls onto greased baking sheets. Spread with the back of a spoon into 3 to 3-1/2 inch rounds. Bake at 350 degrees for 6 to 7 minutes, until edges are golden. Immediately place a paper fortune in center of cookie; fold in half carefully so cookie doesn't flatten. Pick up corners created by fold and fold them together. Place cookies in empty egg carton cups to cool. Makes about 2-1/2 dozen.

Pistachio Thumbprints

1 c. margarine, softened
1/3 c. powdered sugar
1 egg, beaten
1 t. vanilla extract
3/4 t. almond extract
2 c. all-purpose flour
3.4-oz. pkg. instant pistachio
    pudding mix
1 c. pecans, finely chopped
1/2 c. semi-sweet chocolate chips
2 t. shortening

Blend margarine, powdered sugar, egg and extracts. Stir in flour and dry pudding mix. Form dough into one-inch balls; roll in pecans. Place on greased baking sheets; gently press a thumbprint into each. Bake at 350 degrees for 10 to 12 minutes; let cool. Spoon Vanilla Filling into thumbprints. In a plastic zipping bag, microwave remaining ingredients until melted, one to 2 minutes, stirring every 15 seconds. Snip off tip of one corner; drizzle over cookies. Makes 3 dozen.

Vanilla Filling:

2 T. margarine, softened
2 c. powdered sugar
1 t. vanilla extract
2 T. milk

Combine all ingredients; mix well.

**Shawna Green
Dumas, TX**

My good friend, Lisa, is an awesome cook and shared this recipe with me. Everyone raves about these delicious cookies!

253

Giant Chocolate Malt Cookies

1 c. butter-flavored shortening
1-1/4 c. brown sugar, packed
1/2 c. malted milk powder
2 T. chocolate syrup
1 T. vanilla extract
1 egg, beaten
2 c. all-purpose flour
1 t. baking soda
1/2 t. salt
1-1/2 c. semi-sweet chocolate
   chunks
1 c. milk chocolate chips

In a large bowl, blend shortening, brown sugar, malted milk powder, syrup and vanilla for 2 minutes. Add egg; blend well and set aside. Mix together flour, baking soda and salt; gradually blend into shortening mixture. Fold in chocolates; shape dough into 2-inch balls. Arrange 3 inches apart on ungreased baking sheets; bake at 375 degrees for 12 to 14 minutes. Cool on baking sheets for 2 minutes before removing to a wire rack to cool completely. Makes 1-1/2 dozen.

Pat Habiger
Spearville, KS

The next best thing to a good old-fashioned malted shake!

Granny's Chocolate Fudge Cookies

2 6-oz. pkgs. semi-sweet
    chocolate chips
1/4 c. butter
14-oz. can sweetened condensed
    milk
1 t. vanilla extract
1 c. all-purpose flour
1 c. chopped nuts

In a microwave-safe bowl, combine
chocolate chips, butter and
condensed milk. Heat on high
setting until melted, stirring every
30 seconds. Add vanilla, flour and
nuts. Drop by teaspoonfuls onto
greased baking sheets. Bake at
350 degrees for 7 minutes, or until
golden. Cool on wire racks. Makes
5 to 6 dozen.

255

Karen Adams
Cincinnati, OH

My grandmother used to make
these for church dinners.
The food was awesome,
especially these cookies!

Hazelnut Pinwheels

1 c. butter, softened
1 c. sugar
2 egg yolks, beaten
1 t. vanilla extract
1 t. orange extract
1 t. orange zest
2 c. all-purpose flour
1/2 c. chocolate-hazelnut spread

Combine butter and sugar; beat until creamy. Stir in yolks and extracts. Stir in orange zest and flour. Refrigerate dough for 30 minutes. Roll out dough into two, 1/4-inch thick rectangles. Spread with chocolate-hazelnut spread, leaving a 1/4-inch border. Roll up the dough jelly-roll style. Refrigerate another 30 minutes. Slice the rolls into 1/2-inch slices. Arrange slices on ungreased baking sheets. Bake at 350 degrees for 12 to 15 minutes, until edges are slightly golden. Makes about 2 dozen.

Emily Puskac
New Cumberland, WV
Position dental floss under the roll, bring up the floss ends, cross over the center and gently pull to cut the slices...easy!

Rainbow Swirl Cookies

Jamie Johnson
Gooseberry Patch

So pretty and playful! For the most vibrant colors, use gel paste food coloring found in craft stores.

3/4 c. butter, softened
3-oz. pkg. cream cheese,
   softened
1 c. sugar
1 egg, beaten
1 t. vanilla extract
2-3/4 c. all-purpose flour
1 t. baking powder
1/4 t. salt
purple, blue, yellow and pink
   gel paste colorings
12 lollipop sticks

In a bowl, beat butter, cream cheese and sugar until fluffy. Add egg and vanilla; beat until smooth and set aside. Combine flour, baking powder and salt; add to butter mixture. Stir until soft dough forms. Divide dough into fourths. Tint each with a different food color. Wrap in plastic wrap and chill for 2 hours. Roll dough into 3/4-inch balls. For each cookie, place one ball of each color together and roll to make one large ball. Shape into a 12-inch-long rope; starting at one end, coil rope to make a 2-3/4 inch round cookie. Place 3 inches apart on lightly greased baking sheets. Insert lollipop sticks into bottoms of cookies. Bake at 350 degrees for 8 to 10 minutes, until lightly golden. Makes one dozen.

Simple Almond Biscotti

2 c. butter, softened
3/4 c. sugar
2 eggs, beaten
3 T. orange zest
1 t. almond extract
2-1/4 c. all-purpose flour
1-1/2 t. baking powder
1/4 t. salt
3/4 c. slivered almonds, toasted

In a large bowl, beat together butter and sugar; add eggs. Mix in orange zest and almond extract until well blended. Stir in remaining ingredients. On a floured board, divide dough in half; roll and form each half into a 10-inch by 1-1/2 inch roll. Arrange rolls on an ungreased baking sheet 2 inches apart. Bake at 350 degrees for 20 to 25 minutes. Let cool on baking sheet for 5 minutes. Slice each roll diagonally into 1/2-inch thick slices. Lay the slices cut-side down on the baking sheet; bake for an additional 8 minutes. Turn slices over and bake an additional 8 to 10 minutes, until lightly golden. Remove from baking sheet to cool on a wire rack. Makes 2 dozen.

Kelly Alderson
Erie, PA

Enjoy these crisp cookies as an on-the-go breakfast or an after-dinner sweet.

The Ultimate Chip Cookies

2-1/2 c. all-purpose flour
1 t. baking soda
1/2 t. salt
1 c. butter, softened
1 c. brown sugar, packed
1/2 c. sugar
2 eggs, beaten
1 T. vanilla extract
3/4 c. semi-sweet chocolate chips
3/4 c. white chocolate chips
3/4 c. peanut butter chips
3/4 c. candy-coated chocolate
    mini-baking bits
1/2 c. chopped pecans

Combine flour, baking soda and salt; set aside. In a large bowl, beat together butter and sugars until light and fluffy; blend in eggs and vanilla. Mix flour mixture into butter mixture; fold in chips, baking bits and pecans. Drop by tablespoonfuls 2 inches apart onto ungreased baking sheets; bake at 375 degrees for 10 to 12 minutes. Cool on baking sheets for 2 minutes; remove to wire racks to cool completely. Makes about 4 dozen.

Cindy Griffin
Bloomfield, MO
Bursting with flavor, these will be an instant hit!

259

Mint-Chocolate Sandwiches

1/4 c. whipping cream
12-oz. pkg. semi-sweet chocolate
    chips, divided
3/4 t. peppermint extract
2 9-oz. pkgs. chocolate wafer
    cookies

In a small saucepan, bring cream to
a simmer over medium heat. Add
3/4 cup chocolate chips; stir constantly
until melted and smooth. Stir in
extract. Let cool 15 minutes. Spoon
one teaspoon chocolate mixture onto a
wafer cookie; sandwich with another
cookie. Repeat with remaining cookies.
Refrigerate for 10 minutes, or until
firm. Melt remaining chocolate in a
double boiler, stirring constantly. Let
cool slightly. Dip each sandwich into
melted chocolate to coat; shake off
excess. Place sandwiches on a wire rack
set over a baking sheet; refrigerate 15
minutes, or until set. Makes 3 dozen.

Carol Lytle
Columbus, OH
Crunchy, creamy, minty
goodness...yum!

The Best Oatmeal Cookies

1 c. golden raisins
3 eggs, beaten
1 t. vanilla extract
1/2 c. margarine, softened
1/2 c. butter, softened
1 c. brown sugar, packed
1 c. sugar
2-1/2 c. all-purpose flour
1 t. salt
2 t. baking soda
1 T. cinnamon
2 c. quick-cooking oats,
    uncooked
1 c. chopped pecans

261

In a small bowl, combine raisins, eggs and vanilla. Cover with plastic wrap and let stand one hour. In a large bowl, combine margarine, butter and sugars. In a separate bowl, whisk together flour, salt, baking soda and cinnamon. Add flour mixture to margarine mixture; mix until well blended. Stir in raisin mixture, oats and pecans. Dough will be stiff. Drop by rounded teaspoonfuls onto ungreased baking sheets. Bake at 350 degrees for 10 to 12 minutes. Makes 4 dozen.

Trudy Cox
Plano, TX

I just keep this recipe on my e-mail for forwarding to anyone who asks for it! Soaking the raisins is what makes them so special.

Blueberry Linzer Tarts

Cathy Hillier
Salt Lake City, UT
Any flavor of preserves
will work in these
divine cookies!

1-1/4 c. butter, softened
2/3 c. sugar
1-1/2 c. almonds, ground
1/8 t. cinnamon
2 c. all-purpose flour
6 T. blueberry preserves
Garnish: powdered sugar

Blend butter and sugar until light and fluffy. Stir in almonds, cinnamon and flour, 1/2 cup at a time. Cover and refrigerate for about one hour. On a lightly floured surface, roll out half of dough 1/8-inch thick. Cut out 24 circles with a 2-1/2 inch round cookie cutter. Cut out centers of 12 circles with a 1/2-inch mini cookie cutter; leave remaining 12 circles uncut. Arrange one inch apart on ungreased baking sheets. Bake at 325 degrees for 10 to 12 minutes, until golden. Cool completely on a wire rack. Thinly spread preserves over solid circles; sprinkle cut-out cookies with powdered sugar. Carefully sandwich solid and cut-out cookies together. Spoon a little of remaining jam into cut-outs. Makes one dozen.

Buttermilk Sugar Cookies

2 c. sugar
2 c. shortening
4 eggs, beaten
1 T. vanilla extract
2 c. buttermilk
6 c. all-purpose flour
1 T. plus 1 t. baking powder
2 t. baking soda
1/2 t. salt
16-oz. container butter cream
   frosting
Optional: colored sugar
   or sprinkles

263

Blend together sugar, shortening and eggs. Add vanilla and buttermilk. In a separate bowl, combine flour, baking powder, baking soda and salt; stir into sugar mixture. Add more flour as needed to make a firm dough. Chill for 2 to 3 hours or overnight. On a floured surface, roll out dough to a 1/4-inch thickness. Cut out with cookie cutters; place on greased baking sheets. Bake at 350 degrees for 7 to 8 minutes. Let cool. Frost and decorate as desired. Makes about 6 dozen.

Meri Hebert
Cheboygan, MI

I make these for every holiday...they're the softest cookies ever, and everyone always wants the recipe!

Coconut-Lime Macaroons

3 egg whites, beaten
3 c. sweetened flaked coconut
1/4 c. sugar
3 to 4 T. all-purpose flour
1/4 c. lime juice
1 to 2 T. lime zest
1/4 t. vanilla extract

In a large bowl, combine all ingredients thoroughly. Form into one-inch balls and place 1/2 inch apart on lightly greased baking sheets. Bake at 350 degrees for 12 to 15 minutes, until edges are lightly golden. Makes 2 to 3 dozen.

Sharon Demers
Dolores, CO

I experimented and came up with this macaroon alternative. The taste is refreshing and perfect for a summer get-together or ladies' tea.

Macadamia & Chocolate Chip Cookies

2-1/2 c. all-purpose flour
1 t. baking soda
1/2 t. salt
3/4 c. sugar
3/4 c. brown sugar, packed
1 c. margarine
1-1/2 t. vanilla extract
2 eggs, beaten
2 c. extra-large milk chocolate
   chips or chunks
3/4 c. macadamia nuts, chopped
Optional: 1/2 c. sweetened
   flaked coconut

Mix together flour, baking soda
and salt; set aside. In a large bowl,
combine sugars; beat in margarine
and vanilla until fluffy. Add eggs,
mixing well. Add flour mixture to
sugar mixture and beat until well
blended. Stir in chocolate chips,
macadamia nuts and coconut, if
using. Drop by 1/4 cupfuls, 3 inches
apart, onto ungreased baking sheets.
Bake at 375 degrees for 10 to
15 minutes, until golden. Makes
2 to 3 dozen.

265

Elizabeth Arnold
Dallas, OR

A yummy recipe combining
two of my favorites...
milk chocolate and
macadamia nuts!

Italian Cheese Cookies

2 c. sugar
1 c. butter, softened
1 t. vanilla extract
1 t. salt
15-oz. container ricotta cheese
4 c. all-purpose flour
1 t. baking soda

Use an electric mixer on medium speed to blend sugar, butter, vanilla, salt and ricotta cheese. Gradually stir in flour; mix in baking soda. Drop by teaspoonfuls onto ungreased baking sheets. Bake at 350 degrees for 10 to 13 minutes. Cool on wire racks. Spread Sweet Vanilla Icing over cookies. Makes about 4 dozen.

Sweet Vanilla Icing:

2/3 c. plus 1 T. sweetened
    condensed milk
1/2 c. butter, softened
1 t. vanilla extract
2 c. powdered sugar
Optional: red food coloring

Mix all ingredients with an electric mixer on low speed.

Sue Scott
Palmerton, PA

A former co-worker gave me this recipe years ago...it has become one of my husband's favorites!

Baklava Cookies

1/4 c. butter
1/2 c. powdered sugar
3 T. honey
3/4 c. walnuts, finely chopped
1/4 t. cinnamon
1 t. lemon zest
18-oz. pkg. refrigerated sugar
   cookie dough

In a saucepan over low heat, melt butter; stir in powdered sugar and honey. Bring to a boil and remove from heat. Stir in nuts, cinnamon and lemon zest. Let cool 30 minutes. Shape cooled butter mixture into 1/2-inch balls. Divide cookie dough into 24 pieces. Roll each piece of dough into a ball and place 2 inches apart on greased baking sheets. Bake at 350 degrees for 6 minutes. Remove cookies and press a butter-mixture ball into the center of each cookie. Bake an additional 6 to 7 minutes, until edges are golden. Transfer to wire racks and cool completely. Makes 2 dozen.

267

Tara Horton
Delaware, OH

All the wonderful flavor of baklava without all the work!

Twist Cookies

1 c. butter, softened
1-1/2 c. sugar
6 eggs, divided
1 t. vanilla extract
4 t. baking powder
4 to 5 c. all-purpose flour
Optional: sanding sugar

With an electric mixer on high speed, beat butter until fluffy, 4 to 5 minutes. Gradually add sugar, beating another 5 minutes. Add 4 eggs, one at a time, mixing well after each addition; blend in vanilla and baking powder. Gradually mix in flour until a stiff dough forms; roll dough into one-inch balls. Roll each ball into an 8-inch-long rope; fold in half and twist 2 to 3 times. Place on aluminum foil-lined baking sheets; set aside. Beat remaining eggs; brush onto each twist. Sprinkle with sugar, if using. Bake at 350 degrees for 15 to 20 minutes. Makes about 5 dozen.

Virginia Cook
Fairfield, CT

The prettiest cookies... sprinkle with colored sugar for extra sparkle.

Raspberry-Almond Shortbread Cookies

2/3 c. sugar
1 c. butter, softened
2 t. almond extract, divided
2 c. all-purpose flour
1/2 c. seedless raspberry jam
1 c. powdered sugar
2 to 3 t. water

Using an electric mixer on medium speed, combine sugar, butter and 1/2 teaspoon almond extract until creamy. Reduce speed to low and add flour. Continue beating until well mixed. Shape dough into one-inch balls. Place 2 inches apart on ungreased baking sheets. Gently press a thumbprint in center of each cookie. Fill each with about 1/4 teaspoon jam. Bake at 350 degrees for 14 to 18 minutes, until edges are lightly golden. Let cool one minute on baking sheets. Remove cookies to wire racks to cool completely. Combine remaining extract, powdered sugar and water; drizzle lightly over cookies. Makes 3-1/2 dozen.

Dee Ann Ice
Delaware, OH

These buttery-delicious cookies look beautiful on a dessert tray!

Maple Drop Cookies

1 c. butter, softened
3/4 c. sugar
2 c. all-purpose flour
1/4 t. salt
1-1/2 t. maple flavoring
Optional: pecan halves

Beat butter and sugar until light and fluffy; blend in remaining ingredients except pecan halves. Drop by teaspoonfuls onto greased baking sheets; press a pecan half on top of each cookie, if desired. Bake at 350 degrees for 12 to 15 minutes. Makes about 3 dozen.

Debi DeVore
Dover, OH

So easy! Sometimes we frost with cream cheese frosting flavored with a few drops of maple flavoring.

Chocolate-Orange Snowballs

9-oz. pkg. vanilla wafers
2-1/4 c. powdered sugar, divided
1/4 c. baking cocoa
1/4 c. light corn syrup
1/3 c. frozen orange juice
    concentrate, thawed
1-1/2 c. chopped pecans

In a food processor, combine vanilla
wafers, 2 cups powdered sugar,
cocoa, corn syrup and orange juice.
Process until wafers are finely ground
and mixture is well blended. Add
pecans and process until nuts are
finely chopped. Transfer mixture to
a bowl; form into one-inch balls.
Roll in remaining powdered sugar.
Store in an airtight container. Makes
about 5 dozen.

271

Beth Kramer
Port Saint Lucie, FL
I love the flavor combination
of these no-bake snowballs.
I'm in heaven with a cup of
orange and spice tea!

Ice Cream Nut Roll Crescents

4 c. all-purpose flour
2 c. butter, softened
1 pt. vanilla ice cream, softened
3/4 c. milk
2 8-oz. pkgs. walnuts, finely
    chopped
1 c. sugar
1 t. vanilla extract
Garnish: powdered sugar

Combine flour, butter and ice cream.
Form dough into 4 balls; wrap in
plastic wrap and refrigerate 8 hours. In
a saucepan, heat milk just to boiling; let
cool slightly. In a bowl, combine milk,
walnuts, sugar and vanilla; thin with
one to 2 teaspoons milk if too thick.
Turn a dough ball out onto a powdered
sugar-covered surface. Roll dough into
a circle, 1/8-inch thick. Use a pizza
cutter to cut circle into 12 wedges.
Spread about 2 teaspoons walnut
mixture onto each slice; don't overfill.
Starting on the wide end, roll up each
wedge and form into a crescent shape.
Repeat for remaining dough balls.
Arrange crescents on ungreased baking
sheets. Bake at 350 degrees for 18 to
20 minutes. Sprinkle with powdered
sugar while still warm. Let cool. Store
in an airtight container. Makes 4 dozen.

Mel Chencharick
Julian, PA

The ice cream makes
these cookies so rich
and delicious.

Peanut Butter Sandwich Dips

1-1/2 c. all-purpose flour
3/4 t. baking soda
1/4 t. salt
1/2 c. butter, softened
1-1/4 c. creamy peanut butter,
   divided
1 c. sugar
1 egg, beaten
1/4 c. powdered sugar
1 c. semi-sweet chocolate chips
4 t. oil

Whisk together flour, baking soda and salt. In a separate bowl, beat butter, 1/2 cup peanut butter, sugar and egg until smooth. Gradually beat flour mixture into butter mixture. Drop by rounded teaspoonfuls onto ungreased baking sheets. Bake at 350 degrees for 10 minutes, or until puffed. Cool 2 minutes on baking sheets. Remove cookies to a wire rack; let cool. Combine powdered sugar with remaining peanut butter; spread one rounded teaspoon on flat side of half the cookies. Top with remaining cookies. Refrigerate 30 minutes. In a microwave-safe bowl, microwave chocolate chips and oil one minute; stir until melted. Dip cookies halfway into melted chocolate. Let excess drip off. Refrigerate on wax paper-lined baking sheets until set. Makes 3 dozen.

Linda Doyle
West Seneca, NY

My grandchildren love these! I've kept the recipe a secret so they can always enjoy them when they come to visit Grandma & Grandpa.

Molasses Crinkles

3/4 c. shortening
1 c. brown sugar, packed
1 egg, beaten
1/4 c. molasses
2-1/4 c. all-purpose flour
1/4 t. baking soda
1 t. cinnamon
1 t. ground ginger
Garnish: sugar

In a bowl, mix shortening, brown sugar, egg and molasses. Stir in remaining ingredients except garnish in the order listed. Roll dough into one-inch balls. Dip tops in sugar and place on ungreased baking sheets. Gently press a thumbprint into each. Sprinkle one to 4 drops of water in each indentation. Bake at 350 degrees for 10 to 12 minutes. Let cool on a wire rack. Makes 4 dozen.

Patty Fosnight
Childress, TX

These are a favorite of all who taste them. My mother-in-law and I would make them every year to give away with our holiday cookie trays.

Triple-Layered Brownies

20-oz. pkg. brownie mix
3 eggs, beaten
1/4 c. water
1/2 c. oil
16-oz. container cream cheese
   frosting
1 c. creamy peanut butter
12-oz. pkg. milk chocolate chips
2-1/2 c. crispy rice cereal

In a large bowl, stir dry brownie mix, eggs, water and oil just until combined. Grease the bottom of a 13"x9" glass baking pan; pour in batter. Bake at 350 degrees for 27 to 30 minutes. Cool in pan. Spread frosting over cooled brownies; refrigerate until set. In a saucepan, melt peanut butter and chocolate chips together over low heat, stirring frequently until smooth. Remove from heat. Mix in cereal and spread evenly over frosting. Refrigerate until set. Cut into squares. Makes 2 dozen.

Alicia Allen
Lakeside, AZ

I make these cake-type brownies for any get-together. Everyone begs for the recipe! Be sure to use creamy frosting instead of whipped.

Divine Praline Brownies

22-1/2 oz. pkg. brownie mix
1/4 c. butter
1 c. brown sugar, packed
1 c. chopped pecans

Prepare brownie mix according to package directions. Spread in a greased 13"x9" baking pan. Set aside. Melt butter in a skillet over low heat; add brown sugar and pecans. Heat until sugar dissolves; drizzle over brownie mix. Bake at 350 degrees for 25 to 30 minutes. Cool and cut into bars. Keep refrigerated. Makes 12 to 15.

Sandy Bernards
Valencia, CA

Sugar-coated pecans give brownies a delicious new taste!

Gingerbread Brownies

1-1/2 c. all-purpose flour
1 c. sugar
1/2 t. baking soda
1/4 c. baking cocoa
1 t. ground ginger
1 t. cinnamon
1/2 t. ground cloves
1/4 c. butter, melted and slightly
  cooled
1/3 c. molasses
2 eggs, beaten
Garnish: powdered sugar

277

In a large bowl, combine flour,
sugar, baking soda, cocoa and spices.
In another bowl, combine butter,
molasses and eggs. Add butter
mixture to flour mixture, stirring
until just combined. Spread in a
greased 13"x9" baking pan. Bake at
350 degrees for 20 minutes. Cool
in pan on a wire rack. Dust with
powdered sugar. Cut into squares.
Makes 2 dozen.

Stephanie Mayer
Portsmouth, VA

These brownies hit the spot
when I've got a hankering for
gingerbread but don't want
to roll out cookie dough!

Pumpkin Spice & Chocolate Bars

2 eggs, beaten
1/2 c. oil
18-1/2 oz. pkg. yellow cake mix
1 t. pumpkin pie spice
1-1/2 c. semi-sweet chocolate chips
1/2 c. chopped nuts

In a bowl, combine eggs and oil. Stir
in dry cake mix and pumpkin pie spice
until well blended. Fold in chocolate
chips and nuts. Spread into a greased
13"x9" baking pan. Bake at 350 degrees
for 28 to 30 minutes. Cool completely.
Cut into bars. Makes 20.

Kristin Pittis
Dennison, OH

This is a quick & easy
dessert that can be made in
a pinch. The pumpkin pie
spice makes it a little
different from traditional
chocolate chip bars.

Cream Cheese Crescent Bars

2 8-oz. tubes refrigerated
crescent rolls, separated
2 8-oz. pkgs. cream cheese,
softened
1 t. vanilla extract
2/3 c. sugar
1 egg, separated

Line the bottom of a greased
13"x9" baking pan with one package
crescent rolls, pinching seams
together; set aside. Blend together
cream cheese, vanilla, sugar and
egg yolk; spread evenly over crust.
Gently place remaining crescent
roll dough on top, pinching together
seams. In a bowl, whisk egg white
until frothy; brush over dough.
Sprinkle with Cinnamon Topping;
bake at 350 degrees until golden,
about 25 to 30 minutes. Cool; slice
into bars or triangles. Makes 2 dozen.

Cinnamon Topping:

1/2 c. sugar
1/4 c. chopped pecans
1 t. cinnamon

Gently toss together all ingredients.

279

Lisa Delisi
Bristol, WI

I take this dessert to almost
every event I attend...and I
always bring copies of the
recipe because I get so
many requests!

Double Chocolate-Mint Brownies

1 c. all-purpose flour
1 c. sugar
1 c. plus 6 T. butter, softened
   and divided
4 eggs, beaten
16-oz. can chocolate syrup
2 c. powdered sugar
1 T. water
1/2 t. mint extract
3 drops green food coloring
1 c. semi-sweet chocolate chips

Beat flour, sugar, 1/2 cup butter, eggs and syrup in a large bowl until smooth; pour into a greased 13"x9" baking pan. Bake at 350 degrees for 25 to 30 minutes, until top springs back when lightly touched. Cool completely in pan. Combine powdered sugar and 1/2 cup butter, water, mint extract and food coloring in a bowl; beat until smooth. Spread over brownies; chill. Melt chocolate chips and remaining butter in a double boiler; stir until smooth. Pour over chilled mint layer; cover and chill until set. Cut into small squares to serve. Makes about 4 dozen.

Amy Gitter
Omro, WI
These fantastic brownies are rich and chocolatey with a yummy layer of mint.

Red Velvet Bars

18-1/2 oz. pkg. red velvet
   cake mix
2 T. brown sugar, packed
1 t. baking cocoa
2 eggs, beaten
1/2 c. oil
1/2 t. vanilla extract
2 T. water
1 c. white chocolate chips
1/2 c. chopped pecans
Optional: whipped topping,
   additional chopped pecans

281

In a large bowl, combine dry cake
mix, brown sugar and cocoa. Stir in
eggs, oil, vanilla and water. Mix in
chocolate chips and pecans. Spray
a 13"x9" baking pan with non-stick
vegetable spray; spread in batter.
Bake at 350 degrees for 18 to
20 minutes. Cool and spread with
whipped topping and additional
pecans, if using. Cut into bars.
Makes 20.

Judy Jones
Chinquapin, NC
The bars are easy to
fix...plus they're tasty
and pretty!

Rocky Road Brownies

19-1/2 oz. pkg. fudge brownie mix
2 c. mini marshmallows, divided
12-oz. pkg. semi-sweet chocolate
    chips, divided
1 c. dry-roasted peanuts, divided

Prepare brownie mix according to
package instructions; spread in a
greased 13"x9" baking pan. Sprinkle
one cup mini marshmallows, one cup
chocolate chips and 1/2 cup peanuts
over batter. Bake at 350 degrees for
28 to 30 minutes. Remove from oven;
sprinkle with remaining marshmallows,
peanuts and chocolate chips. Let cool
completely before cutting into squares.
Makes 2 to 3 dozen.

Sheryl Whited
Austin, TX

Ooey-gooey and guaranteed
to be the talk of
the potluck!

Mock Lemon Meringue Bars

16-1/2 oz. tube refrigerated sugar
cookie dough
21-oz. can lemon pie filling
8-oz. pkg. cream cheese,
softened
7-oz. jar marshmallow creme
6-oz. container French vanilla
yogurt
8-oz. container frozen whipped
topping, thawed

Break up cookie dough and press
into the bottom of a greased
13"x9" baking pan. Bake at
350 degrees for 20 to 25 minutes,
until edges are golden and center
is set. Let cool completely. Spread
pie filling over crust. In a large bowl,
use a wooden spoon to beat cream
cheese, marshmallow creme and
yogurt until well blended. Fold in
whipped topping. Spread over pie
filling, swirling to resemble meringue
topping. Refrigerate 2 hours. Cut
into bars. Store in refrigerator.
Makes 2 dozen.

283

Cathy Elgin
Saint Louis Park, MN

If you like lemon meringue
pie, you will love these
bars...so easy and
no measuring!

German Chocolate Cookie Bars

1 egg, beaten
1/2 c. margarine, melted and
    cooled
1/2 t. vanilla extract
18-1/2 oz. pkg. German chocolate
    cake mix
1 c. sweetened flaked coconut,
    divided
16-oz. container vanilla frosting

In a large bowl, beat egg, margarine
and vanilla; stir in dry cake mix and
1/2 cup coconut. Spray a 13"x9" baking
pan with non-stick vegetable spray.
Spread batter in pan. Bake at
350 degrees for 25 to 30 minutes.
Cool in pan 10 minutes. Meanwhile,
combine remaining coconut with
frosting. Lightly spread 1/2 cup frosting
over warm bars. Let cool completely;
frost with remaining frosting. Cut into
bars. Makes 20.

Sally Aken-Linke
Norfolk, NE

I like using Mexican-blend
vanilla extract for a richer
flavor. Lightly frosting the
bars while still warm seals
in the moisture...so tasty!

Dorothy's Raisin Bars

1 c. raisins
3/4 c. apple juice
2 T. shortening
1 c. all-purpose flour
1/2 t. salt
1/2 t. baking soda
1/2 t. baking powder
1 t. cinnamon
1/4 t. ground cloves
1/8 t. nutmeg
Optional: 1/4 c. chopped nuts

In a small saucepan over low heat, bring raisins, apple juice and shortening to a boil. Remove from heat and cool. Mix remaining ingredients in a bowl; stir in raisin mixture. Pour into a greased 8"x8" baking pan. Bake at 350 degrees for 35 to 40 minutes; remove from oven and cool. Cut into 2-inch squares; store in an airtight container. Makes 16.

285

Delinda Blakney
Scottshill, TN

This is one of my mom's favorite recipes! Perfect for packing in lunches or taking along on a road trip.

Salted Nut Roll Bars

18-1/2 oz. pkg. yellow cake mix
1 egg, beaten
1/4 c. butter, melted and slightly
　　cooled
3 c. mini marshmallows
10-oz. pkg. peanut butter chips
1/2 c. light corn syrup
1/2 c. butter, softened
1 t. vanilla extract
2 c. salted peanuts
2 c. crispy rice cereal

Combine dry cake mix, egg and
melted butter; press into a greased
13"x9" baking pan. Bake at 350 degrees
for 10 to 12 minutes. Sprinkle
marshmallows over baked crust; return
to oven and bake for 3 additional
minutes, or until marshmallows are
melted. In a saucepan over medium
heat, melt peanut butter chips, corn
syrup, butter and vanilla. Stir in nuts
and cereal. Spread mixture over
marshmallow layer. Chill briefly
until firm; cut into squares. Makes
2-1/2 dozen.

Sandy Groezinger
Stockton, IL

Salty, sweet, crunchy
and gooey...every
bite satisfies!

Coffee Cream Brownies

3 1-oz. sqs. unsweetened baking
  chocolate, chopped
1/2 c. plus 2 T. butter, softened
  and divided
2 eggs, beaten
1 c. sugar
1 t. vanilla extract
2/3 c. all-purpose flour
1/4 t. baking soda
1 t. instant coffee granules
1/3 c. plus 1 T. whipping cream,
  divided
1 c. powdered sugar
1 c. semi-sweet chocolate chips

In a saucepan over low heat, melt
baking chocolate and 1/2 cup butter;
let cool. In a bowl, beat eggs, sugar
and vanilla. Stir in chocolate mixture.
Combine flour and baking soda and
add to the chocolate mixture. Spread
in a greased 8"x8" baking pan. Bake
at 350 degrees for 25 to 30 minutes.
Let cool. In a bowl, stir coffee
granules into one tablespoon cream
until dissolved. Beat in remaining
butter and powdered sugar until
creamy; spread over brownies. In a
saucepan over low heat, stir and melt
chocolate chips and remaining cream
until thickened. Spread over cream
layer. Let set and cut into squares.
Makes one dozen.

287

Jennifer Crisp
Abingdon, IL

Go ahead and serve
with a scoop of
ice cream...so good!

Swirled Peanut Butter Cheesecake Bars

Jen Stout
Blandon, PA

This is a rich and delicious dessert for all cheesecake lovers!

2 c. graham cracker crumbs
1/2 c. butter, melted
1-1/3 c. sugar
2 8-oz. pkgs. cream cheese, softened
1/4 c. all-purpose flour
12-oz. can evaporated milk
2 eggs, beaten
1 T. vanilla extract
6-oz. pkg. peanut butter & milk chocolate chips

Combine cracker crumbs, butter and 1/3 cup sugar. Press into the bottom of an ungreased 13"x9" baking pan. Beat cream cheese, remaining sugar and flour until smooth. Gradually beat in evaporated milk, eggs and vanilla. Reserve one cup cream cheese mixture; spread remaining mixture over crust. Microwave peanut butter & chocolate chips in a microwave-safe bowl on medium for one to 2 minutes; stir until smooth. Stir in reserved cream cheese mixture; pour over bars. Swirl mixtures with a spoon, pulling plain cream cheese mixture up to surface. Bake at 325 degrees for 40 to 45 minutes, until set. Cool on a wire rack; refrigerate until firm. Cut into bars. Makes 20.

Apple Brownies

1/2 c. butter, softened
1 c. sugar
1 t. vanilla extract
1 egg, beaten
1-1/2 c. all-purpose flour
1/2 t. baking soda
1/2 t. baking powder
1/2 t. nutmeg
1 c. apples, cored, peeled and
   chopped
1/2 c. chopped nuts

289

Beat together butter and sugar until fluffy; stir in vanilla and egg. In a small bowl, combine flour, baking soda, baking powder and nutmeg. Add flour mixture to butter mixture and mix thoroughly. Fold in apples and nuts. Spread in a greased 10"x10" baking pan. Bake at 350 degrees for 30 to 35 minutes. Cool and cut into squares. Makes one dozen.

Ann Watson
Leverett, MA

For the tastiest brownies, try using juicy Golden Delicious or tangy Jonagold apples.

Gail's Pumpkin Bars

**Lisa Thomsen
Rapid City, SD**

Dip a mini cookie cutter into cinnamon and lightly press into the frosting... such a pretty touch!

4 eggs, beaten
1 c. oil
2 c. sugar
15-oz. can pumpkin
2 c. all-purpose flour
2 t. baking powder
1 t. baking soda
1/2 t. salt
2 t. cinnamon
1/2 t. ground ginger
1/2 t. nutmeg
1/2 t. ground cloves

Mix together eggs, oil, sugar and pumpkin in a large bowl. Add remaining ingredients and mix well; pour into a greased and floured 18"x12" jelly-roll pan. Bake at 350 degrees for 30 to 40 minutes, until a toothpick comes out clean. Let cool; frost and cut into bars. Makes 1-1/2 to 2 dozen.

Cream Cheese Frosting:

8-oz. pkg. cream cheese, softened
6 T. butter, softened
1 T. milk
1 t. vanilla extract
4 c. powdered sugar

Beat together cream cheese, butter, milk and vanilla; gradually stir in powdered sugar to a spreading consistency.

Scrumptious Cranberry Blondies

1/2 c. butter, softened
1/2 c. sugar
1/2 c. brown sugar, packed
3/4 t. baking powder
1/4 t. baking soda
1/4 t. salt
2 eggs, beaten
1 t. vanilla extract
1 c. all-purpose flour
1/2 c. sweetened dried
   cranberries
1/2 c. white chocolate chips
1 c. fresh cranberries

291

In a large bowl, beat together butter, sugars, baking powder, baking soda and salt. Beat in eggs and vanilla. Mix in flour, dried cranberries and chocolate chips. Line a 9"x9" baking pan with aluminum foil, leaving a few inches on sides for handles; spray with non-stick vegetable spray. Spread dough in pan; lightly press fresh cranberries into dough. Bake at 350 degrees for 25 to 30 minutes, until a toothpick tests clean. Cool; lift foil to remove from pan. Cut into bars. Makes one dozen.

Audrey Lett
Newark, DE

I look forward to when cranberries are in season, just so I can make these yummy blondies!

Peanut Butter Brownies

1 c. creamy peanut butter
1/2 c. butter, softened
2 c. brown sugar, packed
3 eggs, beaten
1 t. vanilla extract
1 c. all-purpose flour
1/2 t. salt

In a large bowl, blend together peanut butter and butter. Beat in brown sugar, eggs and vanilla until light and fluffy. Blend in flour and salt. Spread into a greased 13"x9" baking pan; bake at 350 degrees for 30 to 35 minutes. Cool in pan; frost with Peanut Butter Frosting. Makes 16.

Peanut Butter Frosting:

2 c. creamy peanut butter
1 c. margarine
1 t. vanilla extract
1/8 t. salt
3 to 4 T. whipping cream
2 c. powdered sugar

Blend peanut butter and margarine until fluffy; gradually blend in remaining ingredients until smooth.

Naomi Cooper
Delaware, OH

A nice change of pace from chocolate brownies! Top with chocolate frosting for a whole new taste.

Iced Raspberry Delights

16-1/2 oz. tube refrigerated sugar cookie dough
1-1/4 c. white chocolate chunks, divided
12-oz. jar seedless raspberry jam
1 t. oil

Press dough into the bottom of an ungreased 13"x9" baking pan. Evenly press one cup chocolate chunks into dough. Bake at 350 degrees for 16 to 20 minutes, until lightly golden. Spread jam over crust; bake an additional 10 minutes. Cool completely. Cut into squares or use a cookie cutter to cut into shapes. Combine remaining chocolate and oil in a plastic zipping bag. Microwave 30 to 45 seconds; squeeze bag until chocolate is melted. Snip off tip of one corner and drizzle over bars. Refrigerate until set. Makes 3 dozen.

293

Vickie

These irresistible treats come together easily and make a thoughtful gift for someone special.

Cookies & Cream Brownies

1/2 c. baking cocoa
1/2 c. margarine, melted
3/4 c. sugar, divided
1/2 c. brown sugar, packed
3 eggs, divided
1/2 c. all-purpose flour
1 t. baking powder
1-1/2 t. vanilla extract, divided
12 chocolate sandwich cookies,
   crushed
8-oz. pkg. cream cheese, softened

In a large bowl, combine cocoa, margarine, 1/2 cup sugar and brown sugar; blend well. Add 2 eggs, one at a time, beating well after each addition. Combine flour and baking powder; stir into cocoa mixture. Stir in one teaspoon vanilla and cookie crumbs. Spread into a greased 11"x7" baking pan. In a small bowl, beat cream cheese and remaining sugar, egg and vanilla until smooth. Spoon cream cheese mixture over batter; cut through batter with a knife to swirl. Bake at 350 degrees for 25 to 30 minutes, until a toothpick inserted near the center comes out with moist crumbs. Cool completely. Cut into bars or into circles using a biscuit cutter. Makes 2 dozen.

Mary Gage
Wakewood, CA

Pour a frosty glass
of milk and dig in!

The Best Blondies

1 c. butter, melted and slightly
   cooled
2 c. brown sugar, packed
2 eggs, beaten
2 t. vanilla extract
2 c. all-purpose flour
1/2 t. baking powder
1/4 t. salt
1 c. chopped pecans
1 c. white chocolate chips
3/4 c. toffee or caramel
   baking bits

295

Line the bottom of a 12"x9" baking
pan with parchment paper. Spray
sides of pan with non-stick vegetable
spray and set aside. In a large bowl,
mix together butter and brown sugar.
Beat in eggs and vanilla until smooth.
Stir in flour, baking powder and salt;
mix in remaining ingredients. Pour
into prepared pan and spread evenly.
Bake at 375 degrees for 30 to
40 minutes, until set in the middle.
Allow to cool in pan before cutting
into bars. Makes one dozen.

Elizabeth Cisneros
Chino Hills, CA

For an extra-special dessert,
serve topped with a scoop
of butter brickle ice
cream...delicious!

Gooey Toffee Scotchies

18-1/2 oz. pkg. yellow cake mix
1/2 c. brown sugar, packed
1/2 c. butter, melted and slightly
   cooled
2 eggs, beaten
1 c. cashews, chopped
8-oz. pkg. toffee baking bits

In a bowl, combine dry cake mix, brown sugar, butter and eggs. Beat with an electric mixer on medium speed for one minute. Stir in cashews. Press mixture into the bottom of a greased 15"x10" jelly-roll pan; sprinkle with toffee bits. Bake at 350 degrees for 15 to 20 minutes, until a toothpick tests clean. Cool in pan and cut into bars or triangles. To serve, drizzle with warm Toffee Sauce. Makes about 2-1/2 dozen.

Toffee Sauce:

3/4 c. plus 1 T. dark brown sugar,
   packed
2 T. dark corn syrup
6 T. butter
2/3 c. whipping cream

In a saucepan over medium heat, bring sugar, syrup and butter to a boil. Cook for 2 minutes. Stir in cream and simmer an additional 2 minutes, or until sauce thickens. Keep warm.

Rhonda Reeder
Ellicott City, MD

I'm always looking for desserts with toffee in them. These delectable bars are my new favorites!

Chocolate-Caramel Brownies

21-oz. pkg. brownie mix
16-oz. container milk chocolate
    frosting
6 to 8 T. caramel ice cream
    topping
Optional: chopped nuts

Prepare brownie mix according to package directions. Let cool. Mix together frosting and ice cream topping in a microwave-safe bowl. Microwave on high for 45 seconds; stir and spread over brownies. Top with nuts, if desired. Makes 2 to 3 dozen.

297

Brynne Stevenson
Springfield, OH

What more can I
tell you...these
are wonderful!

Chocolate Chip Cheesecake Squares

2 16-1/2 oz. tubes refrigerated
   chocolate chip cookie dough
2 c. sugar
3 eggs, beaten
2 8-oz. pkgs. cream cheese,
   softened

Slice cookie dough into 1/4-inch thick slices. Arrange half the cookie dough slices in a greased 13"x9" baking pan; press together to form a crust. In a bowl, combine sugar, eggs and cream cheese; beat until smooth. Spread over crust. Arrange remaining cookie dough slices over cream cheese layer. Bake at 350 degrees for 45 minutes to one hour, until golden. Cool; cut into squares. Makes 15.

Cindy Windle
White Hall, AR
Everyone loves this easy-to-make recipe. When I take them to church potlucks and office events, there are never any leftovers!

Staycation Coconut-Lime Bars

2 c. all-purpose flour
1/4 c. sugar
1/8 t. salt
1/2 c. plus 2-1/2 T. butter
4 eggs, beaten
1 c. chopped almonds
2 c. brown sugar, packed
3 c. sweetened flaked coconut
1-1/2 c. powdered sugar
2 T. lime juice
2 t. lime zest

Combine flour, sugar and salt in a bowl. Cut in butter until mixture resembles coarse meal. Press into an ungreased 15"x10" jelly-roll pan. Bake at 350 degrees for 15 minutes, or until golden. Mix eggs, almonds, brown sugar and coconut until well blended; spread over crust. Bake an additional 30 minutes, or until set. Remove pan to a wire rack; loosen the edges with a metal spatula. Meanwhile, use a fork to combine powdered sugar, lime juice and zest. Working quickly, spread powdered sugar mixture over bars while still warm. Let cool and cut into bars. Makes 4 dozen.

299

Joan White
Malvern, PA

A tangy dessert that puts you in the mood for sandy beaches and warm breezes!

Apricot Layer Bars

1-3/4 c. quick-cooking oats,
  uncooked
1-3/4 c. all-purpose flour
1 c. brown sugar, packed
1 c. butter, softened
1/8 t. salt
12-oz. jar apricot preserves

Mix together oats, flour, brown sugar, butter and salt. Press half of mixture into a greased 8"x8" baking pan. Spread preserves over the top; top with remaining oat mixture. Bake at 350 degrees for 35 minutes. Let cool; cut into squares. Makes one to 1-1/2 dozen.

Marilyn Rogers
Port Townsend, WA
A classic recipe...one bite and you'll know why!

Triple Chocolatey Brownies

2-1/4 c. sugar, divided
2-1/2 c. all-purpose flour,
   divided
1/2 c. baking cocoa
1/2 t. salt
1 c. oil
4 eggs, beaten
1 T. vanilla extract, divided
1/2 c. butter, softened
1/2 c. brown sugar, packed
2 T. milk
2 c. semi-sweet chocolate chips,
   divided
1 T. shortening

301

Combine 2 cups sugar, 1-1/2 cups flour, cocoa and salt; add oil, eggs and 2 teaspoons vanilla. Beat with an electric mixer on medium speed for 3 minutes; pour into a greased 13"x9" baking pan. Bake at 350 degrees for 30 minutes; cool. Beat butter, brown sugar and remaining sugar; add milk and remaining vanilla. Blend in remaining flour until smooth and creamy; fold in one cup chocolate chips. Spread mixture over brownies; refrigerate until firm and cut into squares. Melt remaining chocolate chips and shortening in a double boiler; stir until smooth. Drizzle over brownies. Makes 3 dozen.

Valerie Beeching
Paw Paw, MI

Oh, my! There's chocolate in the brownie, the topping and the icing!

Luscious Banana Bars

1/2 c. butter, softened
1 c. sugar
1 egg, beaten
1 t. vanilla extract
1-1/2 c. bananas, mashed
1-1/2 c. all-purpose flour
1 t. baking powder
1 t. baking soda
1/2 t. salt
1/4 c. baking cocoa

Beat together butter and sugar; add egg and vanilla. Blend until thoroughly combined; mix in bananas. Set aside. Combine flour, baking powder, baking soda and salt; blend into banana mixture. Divide batter in half; add cocoa to one half. Pour vanilla batter into a greased 13"x9" baking pan; spoon chocolate batter on top. Cut through batters with a knife to swirl. Bake at 350 degrees for 25 minutes. Cool; cut into bars. Makes 2-1/2 to 3 dozen.

Barbara Buckley
Edwards, MS

Bananas and chocolate are a terrific combination!

Tiger's Eye Brownies

10-oz. pkg. peanut butter chips
1/2 c. margarine
1-2/3 c. sugar
1-1/4 c. all-purpose flour
1/2 t. salt
1/2 t. baking powder
3 eggs, beaten
1 c. dark or semi-sweet chocolate
  chips

In a saucepan over low heat, melt peanut butter chips and margarine together, stirring frequently until smooth. Remove from heat. Stir in remaining ingredients in the order listed. Spread batter in an ungreased 13"x9" baking pan. Bake at 350 degrees for 25 to 30 minutes, until center is set. Let cool and cut into squares. Makes 20.

Nikki Matusiak
Zelienople, PA

These have replaced the usual variety as our family's favorite brownie...delicious!

Baby Rattle Cupcakes

18-1/2 oz. pkg. yellow cake mix
16-oz. container white frosting
red and blue food colorings
24 lollipops, unwrapped
Garnish: large candy sprinkles
Optional: bows

Follow the package instructions to prepare cake mix and bake in paper-lined muffin cups; let cool. Spoon Vanilla Glaze over cupcakes; let stand until set, about 10 minutes. Divide frosting in half; use a few drops of food coloring to tint one half pink and the other half blue. Place each colored frosting in a plastic zipping bag; snip off a tip and pipe designs onto cupcakes. Attach candy sprinkles with a dot of frosting. Insert a lollipop in the side of each cupcake; tie on bows, if desired. Makes 2 dozen.

Vanilla Glaze:

3 c. powdered sugar
3 T. water
2 T. light corn syrup
1/2 t. vanilla extract

Beat all ingredients until smooth.

Tori Willis
Champaign, IL

You can tint the frosting to match Baby's nursery... so sweet!

Birthday Cake Cookies

16-1/2 oz. tube refrigerated sugar
  cookie dough
16-oz. container white frosting
few drops desired food coloring
Garnish: candy sprinkles
10 birthday candles

Shape 1/3 of cookie dough into 10, one-inch balls; press into bottoms and up sides of lightly greased mini muffin cups. Shape remaining dough into 10 equal balls; press into bottoms and up sides of lightly greased regular muffin cups. Bake at 350 degrees; bake mini cookies 8 to 9 minutes; bake regular cookies 10 to 11 minutes. Cool 5 minutes in tins on wire racks. Remove cookies to wire racks; cool completely. Tint the frosting with food coloring. Spread frosting over top and sides of each cookie. Place one mini cookie on top of one regular cookie. Decorate with sprinkles. Press a candle into center of each cookie. Makes 10.

Nancy Wise
Little Rock, AR

I'm the baker in the family and my granddaughter, Hannah, isn't fond of cake. I made these for her eighth birthday and she was tickled pink!

Be Mine Cherry Brownies

18.3-oz. pkg. fudge brownie mix
3 1-oz. sqs. white baking chocolate
1/3 c. whipping cream
1 c. cream cheese frosting
1/4 c. maraschino cherries,
   drained and chopped
1-1/2 c. semi-sweet chocolate chips
1/4 c. butter
Garnish: candy sprinkles

Prepare brownie mix according to package instructions. Line a 13"x9" baking pan with aluminum foil, leaving several inches on sides for handles. Spray bottom of foil with non-stick vegetable spray; spread batter into pan. Bake at 350 degrees for 24 to 26 minutes; let cool. Lift brownies from pan; remove foil. Use a 3-inch heart-shaped cookie cutter to cut brownies. In a microwave-safe bowl, melt white baking chocolate and whipping cream for one to 2 minutes, stirring until chocolate is melted; refrigerate 30 minutes. Stir frosting and cherries into chilled chocolate mixture; spread over brownies. In a microwave-safe bowl, melt chocolate chips and butter for one to 2 minutes, stirring until smooth. Transfer to a plastic zipping bag, snip off a tip and drizzle over brownies. Garnish with sprinkles. Makes 14.

Dana Cunningham
Lafayette, LA
Bake an extra-special Valentine for your sweetie!

Emerald Isle Cupcakes

1-3/4 c. all-purpose flour
2/3 c. sugar
3.4-oz. pkg. instant pistachio
    pudding mix
1-1/2 t. baking powder
1/2 t. salt
2 eggs, beaten
1-1/4 c. milk
1/2 c. oil
1/2 t. vanilla extract
few drops green food coloring
16-oz. container cream cheese
    frosting
Garnish: candy sprinkles

In a bowl, combine flour, sugar, dry pudding mix, baking powder and salt. In another bowl, beat eggs, milk, oil and vanilla; add to flour mixture and mix until well blended. Fill paper-lined muffin cups 2/3 full. Bake at 375 degrees for 20 to 25 minutes, until a toothpick tests clean. Cool in tin on a wire rack. Add a few drops of food coloring to the frosting and frost the cupcakes. Garnish with sprinkles. Makes 1-1/2 dozen.

Jackie Smulski
Lyons, IL

These cupcakes are not only good for St. Patrick's Day but are a refreshing treat to welcome the first day of spring.

Easter Ice Cream Sandwiches

17-1/2 oz. pkg. sugar cookie mix
assorted food colorings
1 pt. vanilla ice cream, softened
Optional: 2 c. sweetened flaked
   coconut

Prepare cookie dough following package instructions. Reserve one cup of dough. Roll out remaining dough on a floured surface 1/4-inch thick. Use a 3-inch egg-shaped cookie cutter to cut dough. Divide reserved dough in thirds; tint with food coloring as desired. Form colored dough into small balls and ropes and arrange on half the cookies. Place on ungreased baking sheets. Bake at 350 degrees for 7 to 9 minutes. Cool on baking sheets one minute; remove cookies to cool completely on wire rack. Position plain cookie on bottom, spread with ice cream and top with decorated cookie. Gently press together; freeze until serving time. If desired, mix a few drops of green food coloring and coconut; let dry on wax paper. Fill a platter or ramekins with coconut. Arrange sandwiches on top. Makes about one dozen.

Anna McMaster
Portland, OR

Wrap these springtime treats in pastel-colored plastic wrap and store in the freezer until ready to serve.

Flowerpot Cupcakes

Thanks, Mom!

Joanna Nicoline-Haughey
Berwyn, PA

These pretty cupcakes
are perfect for
Mothers' Day!

18-1/2 oz. pkg. favorite-flavor
  cake mix
20 flat-bottomed ice cream cones
16-oz. container favorite-flavor
  frosting
Garnish: candy sprinkles
20 lollipops, unwrapped
20 spearmint candy leaves

Prepare cake mix as directed on
package. Fill ice cream cones
3/4 full. Arrange on ungreased
baking sheets or in muffin tins. Bake
at 350 degrees for 18 to 20 minutes.
Let cool completely. Frost cupcakes
and garnish with sprinkles. Insert a
lollipop into the center of each
cupcake. Arrange candy leaves on
frosting at the base of the lollipop
stick. Makes 20.

Bride & Groom Cookies

17-1/2 oz. pkg. sugar cookie mix
Royal Icing (recipe on page 106)

Following package instructions, prepare and bake sugar cookies using a 2-inch heart-shaped cookie cutter; let cool. Spoon one cup each of the Royal Icing and Black Royal icing into separate plastic zipping bags. Seal bags and snip off a tip on each. Referring to photo, pipe outlines of white Royal Icing and Black Royal Icing onto the cookies. Let icing set. Thin remaining icings with a little water and use a spoon to spread the icing on the cookies, filling in the outlines. Makes 2 dozen.

Black Royal Icing:

2 c. powdered sugar
2-1/2 T. baking cocoa
1-1/2 T. meringue powder
black gel paste food coloring
2 to 4 T. warm water

Use an electric mixer to combine powdered sugar, cocoa and meringue powder. Mix in gel paste coloring until desired color. Gradually beat in water until icing is desired consistency. Beat on medium-high speed until glossy, 5 to 7 minutes.

Nola Coons
Gooseberry Patch

I made these for my niece's bridal shower...she was thrilled! You'll find meringue powder and black gel paste food coloring at craft stores.

Dad's Giant Cookie

2-1/4 c. all-purpose flour
1 t. baking powder
1/2 t. salt
1 c. butter, softened
1-1/2 c. brown sugar, packed
1 t. vanilla extract
2 eggs
2 c. milk chocolate chips
16-oz. container chocolate
   frosting
7-oz. tube blue decorator icing
Garnish: milk chocolate chunks,
   mini marshmallows, peanuts

In a small bowl, combine flour, baking powder and salt; set aside. Use an electric mixer on medium speed to beat together butter, brown sugar and vanilla for 5 minutes. Add eggs, one at a time, beating well after each addition. Gradually beat in flour mixture; stir in chocolate chips. Spread batter on a 14" round pizza pan lined with parchment paper. Bake at 375 degrees for 30 to 40 minutes, until golden. Cool in pan for 10 minutes. Transfer to a serving platter to cool completely. Decorate as desired with chocolate frosting and blue icing. Sprinkle edges with garnishes as desired. To serve, cut into wedges. Serves 12.

Elizabeth Blackstone
Racine, WI

What better way to celebrate a big-hearted dad than with a big, hearty cookie?

Fourth of July Lemon Bars

16-1/2 oz. pkg. lemon bar mix
1/4 c. powdered sugar
.68-oz. tube red decorating gel
1/4 c. blueberries

Prepare lemon bars as directed on package; bake in an ungreased 9"x9" baking pan. Cool completely in pan on a wire rack. Cut into 6 rectangular bars. Place bars on a serving plate. Sprinkle with powdered sugar. Pipe stripes across bars with decorating gel. Place 6 blueberries in the top corner of each bar. Makes 6.

Marlene Darnell
Newport Beach, CA

With a few simple decorations, your dessert will be the hit of the picnic!

Scaredy-Cat Cookies

1 c. butter, softened
2 c. sugar
2 eggs, beaten
1 T. vanilla extract
3 c. all-purpose flour
1 c. baking cocoa
1/2 t. baking powder
1/2 t. baking soda
1/2 t. salt
48 pieces candy corn
24 red cinnamon candies

In a bowl, combine butter and sugar. Beat in eggs and vanilla. In a separate bowl, combine flour, cocoa, baking powder, baking soda and salt; gradually add to butter mixture. Roll dough into 1-1/2 inch balls. Place 3 inches apart on lightly greased baking sheets. Flatten with a glass dipped in sugar. Pinch tops of cookie to form ears. For whiskers, press a fork twice into each cookie. Bake at 350 degrees for 7 to 8 minutes, until almost set. Remove from oven; immediately press on candy corn for eyes and cinnamon candies for noses. Remove to wire racks to cool. Makes 2 dozen.

313

**Kay Marone
Des Moines, IA**
Kids love to make and eat these cute Halloween goodies!

Spooky Skull Cupcakes

18-1/2 oz. pkg. white cake mix
12 marshmallows
16-oz. can vanilla frosting
Garnish: mini chocolate-covered
   mints, chocolate chips,
   slivered almonds

Prepare cake mix as package directs; bake in 24 paper-lined muffin cups. Cool. Cut each marshmallow in half from top to bottom. Carefully pull each paper liner partially away from cupcake; tuck a marshmallow half between liner and cupcake to create jaw of skull. Spread frosting over cupcake and marshmallow. Add mints dotted with white frosting for eyes, a chocolate chip for a nose and slivered almonds for teeth. Makes 2 dozen.

John Alexander
New Britain, CT

Get really scary and use
cinnamon candies for
the eyes...yikes!

Tom Turkey Cupcakes

18-1/2 oz. pkg. yellow cake mix
16-oz. container chocolate
   frosting
1/2 c. white frosting
2 11-oz. pkgs. candy corn
Garnish: chocolate sprinkles

Follow the package instructions to prepare cake mix and bake in 24 paper-lined muffin cups. Let cool completely. Frost each cupcake completely with chocolate icing. Spoon or pipe a dollop of icing for the head. Put 5 pieces of candy corn along the back side for the feathers. Place one candy corn on the front of the cupcake for the beak. Sprinkle chocolate sprinkles over the chocolate icing, about halfway. Pipe the eyes above the beak with white frosting. Place a sprinkle in the center of each eye. Makes 2 dozen.

Amy Jones
Graham, NC

I just baked these this year and hope to continue the tradition with my son each Thanksgiving as a special memory.

"Oh, Christmas Tree" Cookies

17-1/2 oz. pkg. sugar cookie mix
several drops green food coloring
Garnish: assorted candy sprinkles

Prepare cookie dough according to package directions; mix in food coloring. Cover and refrigerate 3 hours. On a lightly floured surface, roll dough to 1/4-inch thickness. Cut dough with a 3-inch tree-shaped cookie cutter. Place on ungreased baking sheets. Bake at 350 degrees for 7 to 9 minutes. Immediately cut half the cookies in half vertically; trim bottom of all tree trunks so they are straight. Cool on baking sheets one minute; cool completely on wire racks. Color half the Royal Icing with green food coloring. Spread green icing down cut edge of a half cookie. Press a half cookie to center of a whole cookie; let set. Attach a half cookie to back of the whole cookie. Decorate as desired. Makes about 2 dozen.

Royal Icing:

2 c. powdered sugar
1-1/2 T. meringue powder
2 to 4 T. warm water

Combine powdered sugar and meringue powder. With an electric mixer, gradually beat in water until icing is desired consistency. Beat until glossy, 5 to 7 minutes.

Sarah Oravecz
Gooseberry Patch

These three-dimensional cookies can be adapted to any holiday. Just use your favorite cookie cutter and trim the cookie bottoms so they're straight...how fun!

Frosty the Cupcake

8-1/2 oz. pkg. favorite-flavor
   cake mix
1/2 c. creamy peanut butter
24 round buttery crackers
2 6-oz. pkgs. white baking
   chocolate, coarsely chopped
1 c. mini semi-sweet chocolate
   chips
12 pieces candy corn, yellow
   ends removed
24 pieces red candy-coated
   chocolates
.68-oz. tube red decorating gel
16-oz. container white frosting
Garnish: blue candy sprinkles

Follow the package directions to
prepare cake mix and bake in paper-
lined muffin cups; let cool. Spread
peanut butter over half the crackers;
top with remaining crackers. In a
microwave-safe bowl, melt white
chocolate for one to 2 minutes; stir
until smooth. Dip each sandwich in
chocolate and let excess drip off; set
on wax paper. Immediately place
chocolate chips for eyes and mouth
and candy corn for nose. Place a
candy-coated chocolate on each side
of the face and connect with a line of
red decorating gel. Let set. Frost
cupcakes with frosting and garnish
with sprinkles. Top with a snowman
sandwich. Makes one dozen.

Jo Ann
Almost too cute to eat!
Double this recipe for
your holiday open house.

317

INDEX

INDEX

INDEX

INDEX

Salads

Sandwiches

INDEX

Sides

Soups, Chilis & Stews

U.S. to Metric Recipe Equivalents

Volume Measurements

1/4 teaspoon	1 mL
1/2 teaspoon	2 mL
1 teaspoon	5 mL
1 tablespoon = 3 teaspoons	15 mL
2 tablespoons = 1 fluid ounce	30 mL
1/4 cup	60 mL
1/3 cup	75 mL
1/2 cup = 4 fluid ounces	125 mL
1 cup = 8 fluid ounces	250 mL
2 cups = 1 pint =16 fluid ounces	500 mL
4 cups = 1 quart	1 L

Weights

1 ounce	30 g
4 ounces	120 g
8 ounces	225 g
16 ounces = 1 pound	450 g

Oven Temperatures

300° F	150° C
325° F	160° C
350° F	180° C
375° F	190° C
400° F	200° C
450° F	230° C

Baking Pan Sizes

Square

8x8x2 inches	2 L = 20x20x5 cm
9x9x2 inches	2.5 L = 23x23x5 cm

Rectangular

13x9x2 inches	3.5 L = 33x23x5 cm

Loaf

9x5x3 inches	2 L = 23x13x7 cm

Round

8x1-1/2 inches	1.2 L = 20x4 cm
9x1-1/2 inches	1.5 L = 23x4 cm

Recipe Abbreviations

t. = teaspoon	ltr. = liter
T. = tablespoon	oz. = ounce
c. = cup	lb. = pound
pt. = pint	doz. = dozen
qt. = quart	pkg. = package
gal. = gallon	env. = envelope

Kitchen Measurements

A pinch = 1/8 tablespoon	1 fluid ounce = 2 tablespoons
3 teaspoons = 1 tablespoon	4 fluid ounces = 1/2 cup
2 tablespoons = 1/8 cup	8 fluid ounces = 1 cup
4 tablespoons = 1/4 cup	16 fluid ounces = 1 pint
8 tablespoons = 1/2 cup	32 fluid ounces = 1 quart
16 tablespoons = 1 cup	16 ounces net weight = 1 pound
2 cups = 1 pint	
4 cups = 1 quart	
4 quarts = 1 gallon	

Our Story

Back in 1984, we were next-door neighbors raising our families in the little town of Delaware, Ohio. Two moms with small children, we were looking for a way to do what we loved and stay home with the kids too. We had always shared a love of home cooking and making memories with family & friends and so, after many a conversation over the backyard fence, **Gooseberry Patch** was born.

We put together our first catalog at our kitchen tables, enlisting the help of our loved ones wherever we could. From that very first mailing, we found an immediate connection with many of our customers and it wasn't long before we began receiving letters, photos and recipes from these new friends. In 1992, we put together our very first cookbook, compiled from hundreds of these recipes and, the rest, as they say, is history.

Hard to believe it's been over 25 years since those kitchen-table days! From that original little **Gooseberry Patch** family, we've grown to include an amazing group of creative folks who love cooking, decorating and creating as much as we do. Today, we're best known for our homestyle, family-friendly cookbooks, now recognized as national bestsellers.

JoAnn & Vickie

One thing's for sure, we couldn't have done it without our friends all across the country. Each year, we're honored to turn thousands of your recipes into our collectible cookbooks. Our hope is that each book captures the stories and heart of all of you who have shared with us. Whether you've been with us since the beginning or are just discovering us, welcome to the **Gooseberry Patch** family!

Visit us online:
www.gooseberrypatch.com
1•800•854•6673